MONROE

Christmas 1988
Darling Emma
Merry Christmas,
Much love,
Brian
x

JAMES SPADA
With George Zeno

MONROE
Her Life in Pictures

SIDGWICK & JACKSON
LONDON

Books of Related Interest by James Spada

BARBRA: THE FIRST DECADE– —
The Films and Career of Barbra Streisand
THE FILMS OF ROBERT REDFORD
STREISAND: THE WOMAN AND THE LEGEND

ACKNOWLEDGMENTS

Special thanks, once again, to Karen Swenson for her
research help and dedication.

For their help, advice, and enthusiasm, appreciation
to Lindy Hess, Larry Alexander, Doug Bergstreser, Dan
Conlon, Chris Nickens, Lou Valentino, Pat Miller, Neal
Peters, Andre de Dienes, Lester Glassner, Bruce
Mandes, John Liscio, Rick Carl, Mrs. Eunice Murray
Blackmer, Allan Grant, Edward Weston, Mrs. Philippe
Halsman, Margaret Wagstaff, Robb Carr, Dana Berger,
Bill Chapman.

Love to our editor, Laura Van Wormer, and our
agent, Kathy Robbins, who are everthing an author
could hope for.

And a debt of gratitude to all those photographers,
famous and anonymous, who captured the Monroe
image on film and without whom books like this would
be impossible.

First published in Great Britain in 1982
by Sidgwick and Jackson Limited

Reprinted November 1982

This paperback edition first published in June 1983
by Sidgwick and Jackson Limited

Reprinted March 1984
Reprinted November 1985
Reprinted September 1986
Reprinted January 1987
Reprinted November 1987

Originally published in the United States of America
in 1982 by Doubleday and Company, Inc.

Copyright © 1982 by James Spada and George Zeno

ISBN 0-283-98998-X
Printed in Great Britain by
R. J. Acford, Industrial Estate, Chichester, Sussex
for Sidgwick and Jackson Limited
1 Tavistock Chambers, Bloomsbury Way
London WC1A 2SG

Dedicated to my father,
Joseph V. Spada,
who always encouraged me
in my love for Marilyn.

—J.S.

Dedicated to my father,
Jorge; my mother, Alejandrina;
and my sister Vilma,
for their love and understanding.

—G.Z.

Contents

Preface   *x*

Part One
THE EARLY YEARS 1926–1945   *1*

Part Two
STARLET 1946–1950   *13*

Part Three
THE LATEST BLONDE 1951–1952   *35*

Part Four
PHENOMENON 1953–1955   *65*

Part Five
THE NEW MARILYN 1956–1957   *107*

Part Six
ACCLAIM 1958–1959   *137*

Part Seven
DECLINE 1960–1962   *157*

Preface

No other movie star in the seventy years of Hollywood history has ever captured the imagination of the American public quite the way Marilyn Monroe has.

She starred in just eleven films over ten years, not a prodigious output of product compared to that of many other screen greats. But her films were just one part of the Monroe mystique; she was a total celebrity, one in whom the public's interest did not flag despite often lengthy periods between films.

Her rise to fame in the early 1950s was a cultural phenomenon; barely a day passed when one of the New York newspapers wasn't featuring a Monroe photo, article, gossip column item, or all three. The public found her fascinating: she was a beautiful, successful woman who had spent an abysmal childhood dreaming of stardom; she played dumb blondes, yet was famous for her fast witticisms; she was in many ways vulnerable and naïve, yet had a streak of independence and ambition that would surprise many who tried to take easy advantage of her.

Her sexuality was often blatant, yet always there was a childlike innocence about her, a suggestion of the little girl dressed in her mother's clothes and play-acting allure. The playfulness she brought to sex made her carnality at once more stimulating to men and less threatening to women.

She would become, however, Hollywood's ultimate victim, a sensitive, insecure, frightened woman who believed her looks and sexuality were her only key to happiness. Once worldwide fame and adulation had come to her, she realized they were only a partial fulfillment. But by then it was too late to achieve happiness anywhere else—Marilyn Monroe was public property. Her enormous fame destroyed one of her marriages, and the neuroticism that her fame created in her destroyed the other. She was unable to accept happiness from one man, and the love of the masses was merely an empty, temporary tonic.

It has been said of Monroe that her one lasting love affair was with the camera. If that is so, the lens was certainly an ardent paramour. She may have been the most photographed woman of all time; cameramen were present to record her most personal tragedies as well as her most glorious triumphs.

This book might well be considered the history of Marilyn Monroe's love affair with the camera. Although dozens of books have been published about her, none has ever attempted to tell the entire story purely through photographs. In doing so, one inevitably recaptures an era as well as a woman. For Monroe was both a perfect reflection of her time and, in many ways, ahead of it.

This book is, by necessity, primarily about the *public* Marilyn. There is no shortage of recent books purporting to reveal the most intimate details of the private woman. An interest sparked by this book can be more than satisfied by a visit to the nearest library. But it is valuable, I think, to take a look back at *how* Marilyn Monroe made her mark on the world's consciousness, and to re-create the tumultuous excitement her existence generated over the more than ten years that she was a celebrity.

For those who lived through it, I hope this book will revive pleasant memories. For those too young to have experienced Marilyn's life, I think the following pages will at least partially explain why, twenty years after her death, she still fascinates. As for me, it is completely gratifying that the thirteen-year-old president of the Marilyn Monroe Memorial Fan Club can grow up to do a book on his dream girl. That there is still enough interest in Marilyn in the 1980s to make a book like this feasible is the ultimate indication of the extraordinary Monroe magic.

James Spada
Hollywood, California
January 1982

Part One

The Early Years

1926-1945

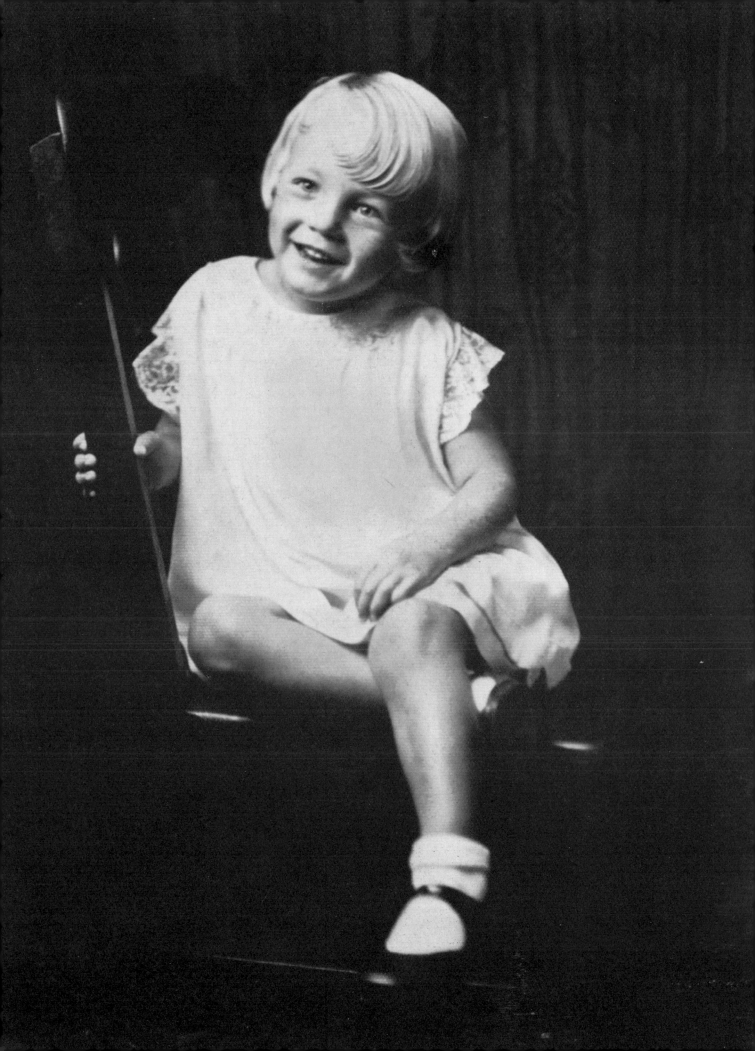

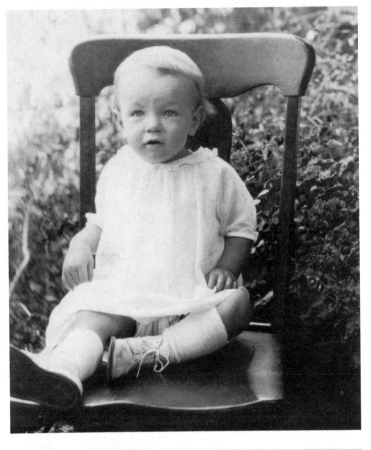

T here are no sweet memories of childhood, no misty tableaux of family, love, and hearth. Instead, there are desertion, madness, attempted murder, child rape. And in the middle, a strange, quiet, unwanted child whose first and most powerful lesson was that the less she said, the less trouble she'd get into.

Norma Jeane Baker was born on June 1, 1926. Her mother, a star-struck Hollywood film cutter, named her after a glamorous movie actress, Norma Talmadge. The last name was a convenience; Gladys Pearl Monroe had been deserted by her husband, Mr. Baker, three years before Norma Jeane's birth, and her second husband, Edward Mortenson, left her when she told him about the pregnancy. Edward Mortenson may have been Norma Jeane's father, but more likely it was a co-worker of Gladys' at the RKO studios, a man she never married.

Gladys Baker's parents and brother had all been mentally ill, and her bad luck with men and the strain of caring for Norma Jeane sent her over the brink. She suffered fits of hysteria and was committed to a mental institution in 1934. Eight-year-old Norma Jeane was treated as though she had no living parents.

From this point on, the child was shunted from one place to another. There were stays in an orphanage, with a guardian, and with eleven sets of foster parents, people who took her in only because the government, at the height of the Depression, paid them to do so. One family made her bathe in water six others had used first;

ABOVE Norma Jeane Baker at eighteen months, 1927.

LEFT Gladys Baker and her two-year-old on an outing, 1928.

OPPOSITE By five, a loveliness began to emerge in the girl. But Marilyn would later say, "No one ever told me I was pretty when I was a little girl. All little girls should be told they're pretty, even if they aren't."

another made her wash hundreds of dishes for five cents a month. "They had kids of their own," she recalled, "and when Christmas came there was a big tree and all the kids in the house got presents but me. One of the other kids gave me an orange. I can remember that Christmas Day, eating that orange all by myself."

By the age of eight she was a pretty girl. Her latest foster parent ran a boardinghouse. One of the boarders, a distinguished older man, told her they would play a game. Instead, he molested her, and when she tried to tell her foster parent, she was slapped and told not to tell lies. It was at that point that she began to stammer.

By the time she reached puberty her psyche was a tender mass of scar tissue. But she was becoming beautiful, and she was developing womanly attributes. She soon discovered that boys gave her the attention she had craved all her life. She began to work at making sure they continued to find her interesting.

ABOVE With friends, at eight years old in Los Angeles. By the age of ten, she had reached almost her adult height and was so thin that classmates called her Norma Jeane, the Human Bean. When she appeared in school productions, she always played "the boy parts." But by the time she was twelve, her figure began to fill out, and she was precociously curvaceous by thirteen.

OPPOSITE With her classmates at Van Nuys High School in a suburb of Los Angeles. She excelled only in English and in attracting appreciative stares from the boys around her. She left during her sophomore year in order to marry James Dougherty, a neighbor she had known for several years.

RIGHT Gladys Baker Ely, photographed in 1963.

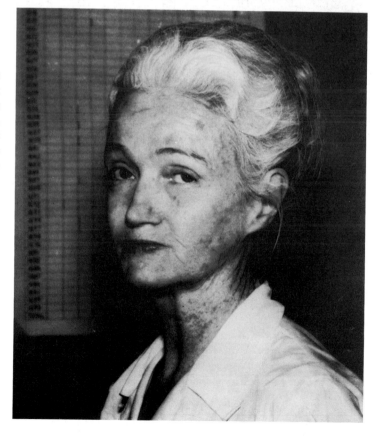

OPPOSITE Mr. and Mrs. James Dougherty on Catalina Island after Jim joined the service, 1944. They had been married in June of 1942, shortly after Norma Jeane's sixteenth birthday. For her it was a marriage of convenience, a way to avoid going back to the orphanage when her guardian at the time could no longer keep her. "But there were other considerations," she said, "just being in love with love or sex or whatever you want to call it." Dougherty insists that his wife was head over heels in love with him, that she threatened to jump off the Santa Monica Pier if he left her. Later he would write: "She has told the press that our marriage was one of expedience, that she was never happy with me. I wonder if she has forgotten how much in love we were." Dougherty describes his wife as blissfully happy, a contented homemaker; she talked of boredom and despair, of hating the housewifely role, and of attempting suicide.

During the same trip to Catalina, Norma Jeane visits a bird sanctuary.

Alone most of the time, with Jim away, Norma Jeane grew restless. In 1944, with the country at war, she got a job in a plane parts factory, spraying fuselages. Jim didn't approve of her wearing sweaters, because their effect on the men around her was inordinate. When he was away, she wore sweaters all the time—when she wasn't wearing other equally revealing outfits.

Norma Jeane Dougherty, model. If the little girl was never told she was pretty, the older girl was. In 1945 army photographer David Conover, snapping pictures of home-front girls working to support the war effort, saw her and asked, "Where have you been all my life? Have you got a sweater?" His pictures prompted the developer at Eastman Kodak to inquire, "Who's your model, for goodness' sake?"

She agreed to be paid five dollars an hour only if her pictures were sold to magazines. Quite a few were. Soon she was working for Emmeline Snively, founder of the Blue Book Models School. "The graduate I'm most proud of," Miss Snively later wrote, "is Marilyn Monroe. Not only because she is the most successful and well known of my students, but because she started with the least. She was cute-looking, but she knew nothing about carriage, posture, walking, sitting, or posing."

Miss Snively told Norma Jeane she'd look much better if she lowered her smile and straightened and bleached her hair. She practiced the smile but resisted dyeing her hair, fearing it would look unnatural. But when she was told that more jobs would come her way as a blonde, she relented. Her first job after the transformation was a shampoo ad (bottom). It was never used.

Part Two

Starlet

1946-1950

The movie career begins. Her success as a model for photographers like Conover and Andre de Dienés resulted in five magazine covers in one month in 1946 and led Howard Hughes to request a screen test. Emmeline Snively got Norma Jeane an agent, who felt she would do better testing with Twentieth Century-Fox. Although the test was shot without Twentieth head Darryl Zanuck's approval (an unheard-of breaking of the rules), Zanuck was impressed. "It's a damn good test," he said after it was included in a day's rushes. "Sign her up." She got her first Fox contract in September 1946. What impressed Zanuck the most was what Billy Wilder would later describe as "flesh impact": "Some girls have flesh that photographs like flesh. You feel you can reach out and touch it."

Divorced from James Dougherty, her name changed to Marilyn Monroe (after actress Marilyn Miller and her mother's maiden name), she became one of dozens of young contract players at Fox. She posed for endless publicity pictures, including one series to accompany the story that she had been a baby-sitter discovered by a Fox talent scout. Said Marilyn later: "They could at least have had me be a daddy sitter."

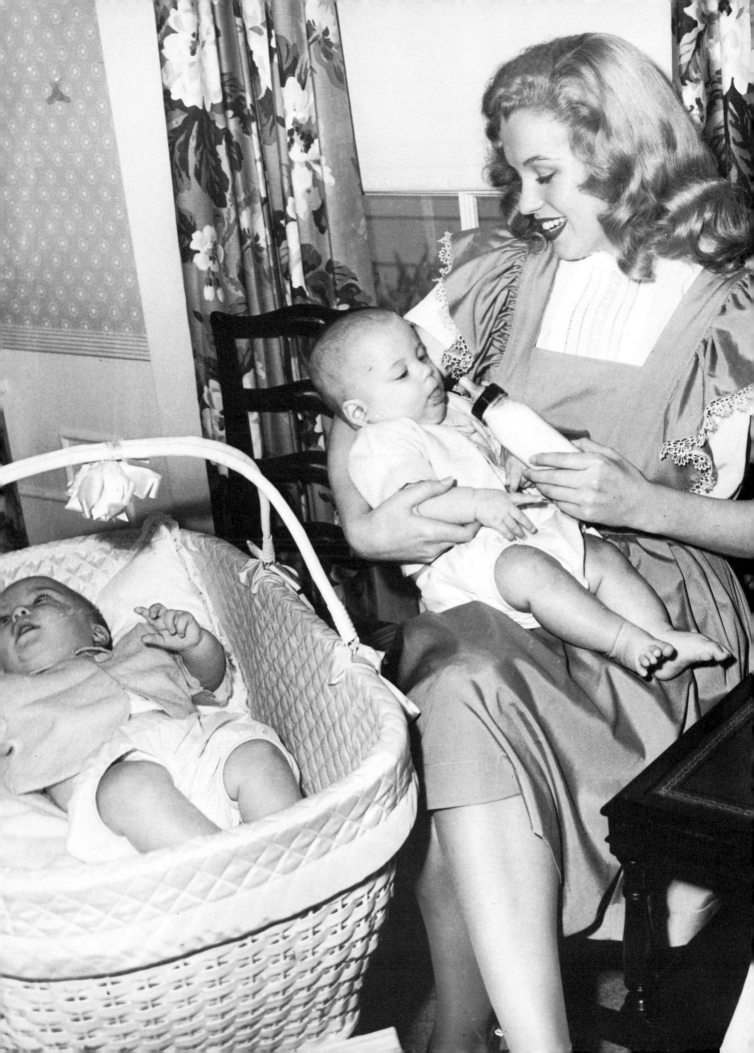

OPPOSITE To publicize the Fox Studio Club annual golf tournament, the "lovely starlet" poses with Henry Fonda, July 1947.

On the set of her first film, *Scudda Hoo! Scudda Hay!*, in which she was to utter one word ("Hi!") to the film's star, June Haver. The word wound up on the cutting-room floor, but she can be glimpsed fleetingly in the scene. The movie was released in early 1948.

Marilyn's second chance, a role as a waitress in *Dangerous Years,* resulted in her first screen close-up, but little else. The film was released before *Scudda Hoo! Scudda Hay!,* on December 8, 1947. After she completed her few scenes, Fox let her option lapse.

OPPOSITE Six months later, Columbia Pictures put her under contract and gave her a sizable role in a B picture, *Ladies of the Chorus.* She played a stripper and sang several songs—including the catchy tune "Every Baby Needs a Da-Da-Daddy." She got her first review on October 23, 1948, and it was a good one. The *Motion Picture Herald* critic wrote: "One of the brightest spots is Miss Monroe's singing. She's pretty, and with her pleasing voice and style, shows promise." Columbia disagreed, and they, too, let her contract expire. She was disappointed but, she would later say, she didn't blame them. "I think if other girls know how bad I was when I started they'll be encouraged," she said. "I finally made up my mind I wanted to be an actress and I was not going to let my lack of confidence ruin my chances." Shunned by films for the time being, she went back to modeling.

No longer under contract to anyone, Marilyn heard about a part for a sexy blonde in the new Marx Brothers movie, *Love Happy*, and arranged to audition for Groucho. She didn't have to do much. "There were three girls there, and Groucho had us each walk away from him," Marilyn said. "I was the only one he asked to do it twice. Then he whispered in my ear, 'You have the prettiest ass in the business.' I'm sure he meant it in the nicest way. I was only supposed to walk in the movie, but Groucho said he would write some special lines just for me." Even with the lines, her screen time was about ninety seconds.

OPPOSITE Her first publicity tour—in 1949, to promote the future release of *Love Happy*— brought her to New York for the first time. She thought that New York was always cold, just as Los Angeles is always warm. She packed nothing but heavy woolen clothes and arrived in the midst of a brutal August heat wave. Lester Cowan, the PR man who accompanied her, had the bright idea of photographing her with ice cream cones to cool off. A close look at this picture reveals the cones as obvious impostors. "It was so hot," Marilyn said, "I spent the rest of the visit in a cotton dress Lester got at a wholesale house."

Wearing the cotton dress, Marilyn takes part in a *Photoplay* publicity stunt—the housewarming for a "Dream House" won by one of the magazine's lucky readers. Here Marilyn, Lon McCallister, and Don DeFore demonstrate the miracle product of one of the manufacturers whose sponsorship made the "Dream House" promotion possible.

OPPOSITE Marilyn is attended to on the set of *A Ticket to Tomahawk*, a quickie Western she did for Fox without a contract in 1949. She appeared in a chorus for one number with the film's star, Dan Dailey.

When she returned to Hollywood after her trip East, Marilyn met Johnny Hyde at a poolside party in Palm Springs. He was quite a bit older than she, a powerful agent, and he soon became her mentor and lover. "Johnny was marvelous, he really was," Marilyn told her first biographer, Maurice Zolotow. "He believed in my talent. He listened to me when I talked, and he encouraged me. He said I would be a very big star."

Hyde was deeply in love with her, and he begged her to marry him. She refused. "I loved him dearly, but I wasn't in love with him. He was a dear friend, a gentle, kind, brilliant man, and I had never known anyone like him."

If she had indeed married Jim Dougherty without loving him, she was not going to make the same mistake again. Hyde, in poor health with a bad heart, told her he didn't have long to live and his happiness would not be complete unless she married him. Besides, he told her, as his wife she would inherit his wealth, in excess of $1 million. She turned him down, and later again as he lay in a hospital after suffering a heart attack. At his funeral she became hysterical and threw herself on his coffin sobbing. His family refused to allow her to sit in the front row with them. She later wrote: "I cried night after night. Sometimes I felt wrong in not marrying him and giving him what he wanted. But I also knew it would be wrong to marry someone you didn't really love. I didn't regret the million dollars I had turned down. I never stopped regretting the loss of Johnny Hyde."

Shortly before his death in 1949, Johnny Hyde arranged for Marilyn to audition for a role in John Huston's film *The Asphalt Jungle*. This was big-time, and Marilyn was nervous. "They're looking for a girl with big bazooms," Marilyn told her friend Jim Bacon. "Johnny told me to dress sexy." She wore falsies stuffed with tissue paper in order to improve on nature. John Huston's first action when he saw her was to reach down her bosom and pull out the tissue paper. "Now we'll read for the part," he said. She asked to read lying on the floor because there wasn't a couch and the part called for much reclining. When she finished, she insisted on doing it again, although Huston said she didn't have to. He gave in, then told her, "You didn't have to read twice. You had the part the first time. You're on salary as of Monday. I want you on the set by nine o'clock, kid."

OPPOSITE Marilyn played Louis Calhern's "niece" in the brutally realistic MGM crime drama, considered one of the all-time great films. Her reviews were excellent, and she would later say she considered it the best acting job she'd ever done. The reactions of preview audiences to her small part were extraordinary; hundreds of cards were filled out asking "Who's the blonde with Calhern?" (Someone had neglected to include her name in the credits.) She began to get a good deal of press attention, but MGM's production chief Dore Schary didn't think she "looked" like a movie star and MGM already had a blonde with pretty fair credentials—Lana Turner. Schary didn't sign Marilyn to a contract.

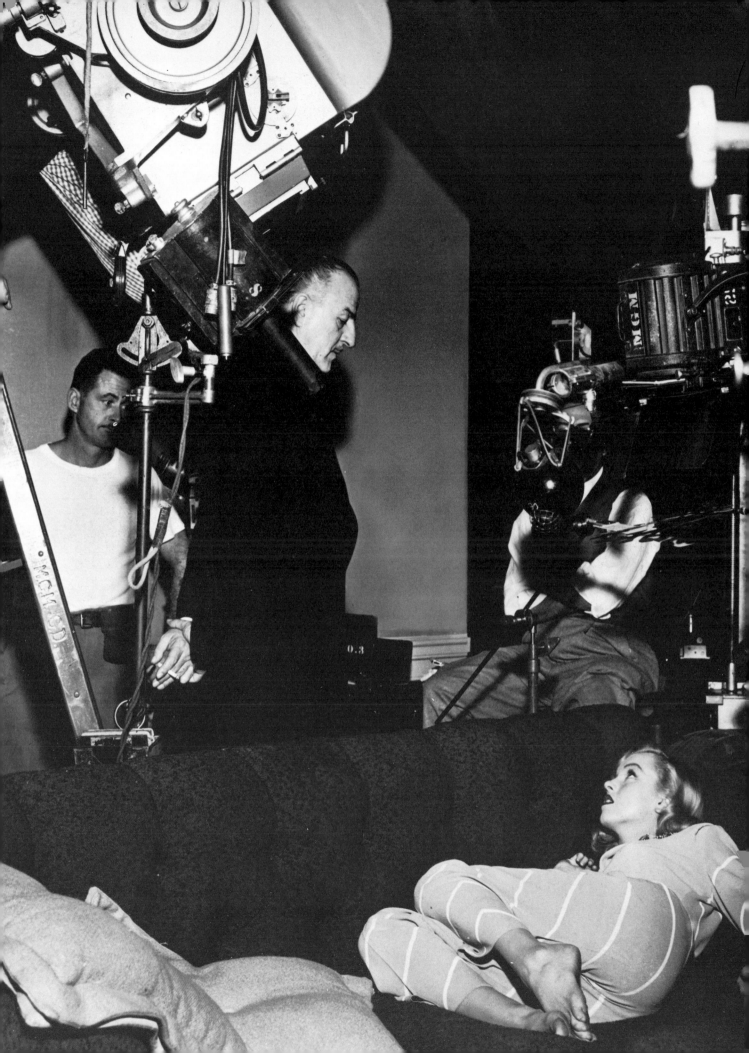

OPPOSITE On the set of *The Fireball*, a 1950
Mickey Rooney epic in which she had a walk-on.

An unusual look at Marilyn, 1950.

With cameraman Milton Krasner on the set of *All About Eve,* 1950. It was another prestigious film for Marilyn, a Joseph Mankiewicz production for Fox starring Bette Davis, Gary Merrill, Anne Baxter, George Sanders, and Celeste Holm. "She was terribly shy," Celeste Holm recalled. "In fact, she was scared to death. She was playing in a pretty big league, you know, but Joe relaxed her into it." Her fright resulted in the first known instance of her famous need for numerous retakes and her renowned lateness. One short scene required twenty-five retakes because she couldn't get her lines right, and she was an hour late her first day on the set.

Marilyn would later say about her chronic lateness: "I guess people think that why I'm late is some kind of arrogance, and I think it is the opposite of arrogance.... I do want to be prepared when I get there to give a good performance or whatever to the best of my ability."

Her performance as Miss Caswell, a graduate of the Copacabana School of Dramatic Art, was funny and realistic, and it impressed Darryl Zanuck. "Put that girl under contract," he ordered when he saw the rushes. He was told she had been under contract and was dropped. "I don't care," he responded. "Bring her back."

Another bit part, in *Right Cross* with Dick Powell (1950), allowed her to act the sophisticate.

BELOW Monroe as she appeared in *Home Town Story,* an hour-long industrial film that also featured Alan Hale, Jr. It was released in May of 1951.

OPPOSITE Despite her appearances in two major films and her new Fox contract, Marilyn was offered no more roles in 1950. She spent her time studying acting and posing for pinups in cocktail dresses and bathing suits, and in outfits like this, commemorating various holidays. Her bathing suit art soon captured the imaginations of newspaper editors, servicemen, and connoisseurs of feminine beauty everywhere, and their response was phenomenal. Before long the Twentieth Century-Fox mailroom was receiving more requests for pictures of Marilyn than of any other Fox player—and she wasn't featured in any current movies. Zanuck suspected that someone was tampering with the mail figures in an effort to promote Marilyn—but when he was convinced that wasn't so, he ordered her put into any Fox picture requiring a beautiful blonde. Marilyn Monroe's career was about to take off.

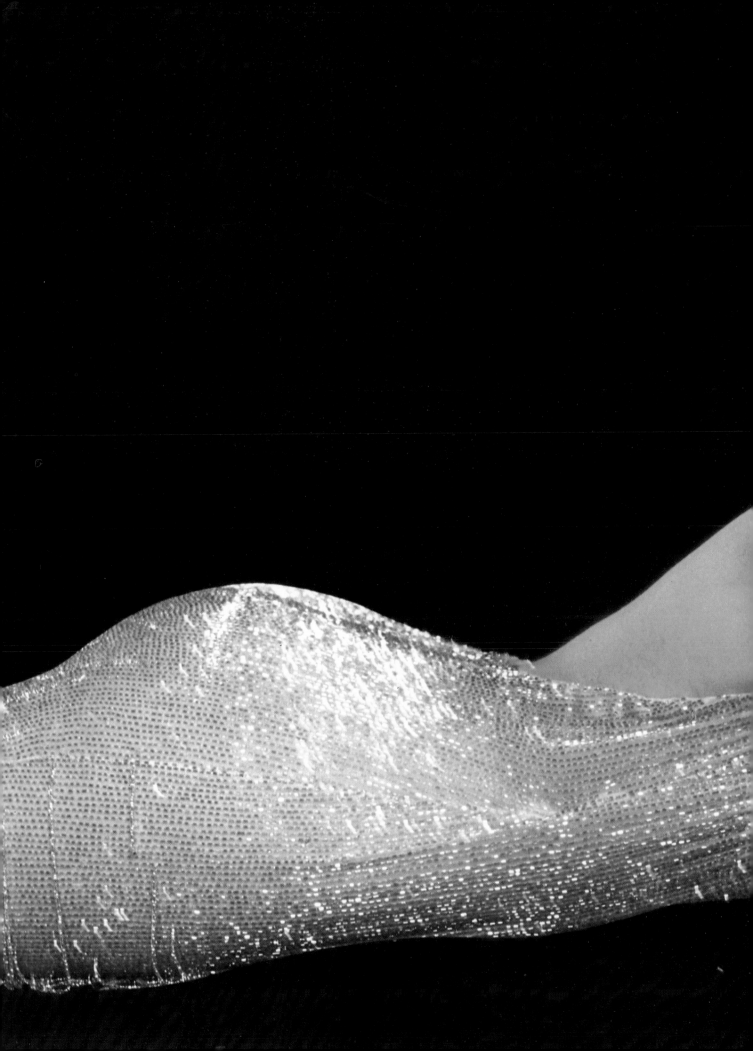

Part Three

The Latest Blonde

1951-1952

The photo's caption read: "Chicago White Sox pitcher Joe Dobson checks over film starlet Marilyn Monroe's form, as outfielder Gus Zernial does the catching. Marilyn, a long-time baseball fan, got some pointers when she visited the Chicago team at their training camp." Marilyn Monroe, of course, didn't know a fast ball from a catcher's mitt, and the photo was only one of the blizzard of publicity photos she posed for. But it would prove extremely significant: baseball immortal Joe DiMaggio saw it in his local newspaper and inquired, "Who's the blonde?"

OPPOSITE Marilyn attends the 1951 Academy Awards, where she presented the Oscar for Achievement in Sound Recording to Thomas Moulton for *All About Eve*.

Marilyn made *Love Nest* in 1951, playing an unwitting temptress who comes between William Lundigan and wife June Haver. She had a few scenes with another newcomer, Jack Paar. "Looking back," Paar wrote in his autobiography, "I guess I should have been excited, but I found her pretty dull. Marilyn spoke in a breathless way which denoted either passion or asthma. She wore dresses with the necklines so low she looked as though she had jumped into her dress and caught her foot on the shoulder straps....She used to carry around the books of Marcel Proust, with their titles facing out, although I never saw her read any of them. She was always holding up shooting because she was talking with someone on the phone. Judging from what's happened, though, I guess she had the right number."

Production Test

6/14/51

Marilyn Monroe

Robert Wagner

TEST STAGE

DO NOT REMOVE

Taking a break from shooting *Love Nest.* Her bathing suit, described by one wit as having "barely enough room for the dots," caused a sensation around the studio lot, and anyone who could make an excuse to be around when Marilyn was filming did so. Finally it got so disruptive the director barred visitors from the set. Zanuck, though skeptical about Marilyn's potential as a major star, couldn't deny her impact on people. He said, "Miss Monroe is the most exciting new personality in Hollywood in a long time." When her contract expired, he re-signed her to a seven-year pact, beginning at $500 a week and escalating semiannually to a ceiling of $1,500 per week. Marilyn was joyous, and confident that Fox now believed in her potential as an actress and a star.

OPPOSITE But the studio continued to put her into silly Grade B comedies, always playing somebody's dumb blond secretary. One of these "classics" was called *Let's Make It Legal,* and as part of her job MM "costarred" in the screen test of another young hopeful, Robert Wagner.

The roles may not have been memorable, but Marilyn was, and her brief appearances in minor films like *As Young As You Feel* were at least promoted prominently.

Marilyn wins the 1951 Henrietta Award as Most Promising Personality of the Year. It has to be the world's most unwieldy award; and Marilyn's gown, one of the world's skimpiest.

OPPOSITE Marilyn was "loaned" to RKO in 1951 for a relatively significant dramatic role in Clifford Odets' *Clash by Night,* costarring Barbara Stanwyck, Paul Douglas, and Robert Ryan. Monroe received equal billing with the stars and most of the attention during filming. Douglas complained bitterly about it one day: "Why the hell don't these photographers ever take any pictures of us? It's always that goddamn blond bitch." Barbara Stanwyck responded, "It's this way, Paul—she's younger and more beautiful than any of us."

Marilyn took her dramatic opportunity in the film quite seriously. For the first time her drama coach, Natasha Lytess, accompanied her onto the set, and Monroe demanded retakes whenever Lytess disapproved, regardless of whether director Fritz Lang was happy with the take or not. Lang ordered Lytess off the set, and MM refused to work without her. Finally, a compromise: Lytess would stay, but she could not contradict any of Lang's directives.

Marilyn's perfectionism paid off—she received her best reviews ever for *Clash by Night.* Alton Cook of the New York *World-Telegram and Sun* wrote: "Before going any further with a report on *Clash,* perhaps we should mention the first full-length glimpses the picture gives us of Marilyn Monroe as an actress. The verdict is gratifyingly good…this girl has a refreshing exuberance, an abundance of girlish high spirits. She is a forceful actress, too, when crisis comes along. She has definitely stamped herself as a gifted new star, worthy of all that fantastic press agentry. Her role is not very big, but she makes it dominant."

Her barely apparent dress at the Henrietta Awards stirred up the first of many controversies around Monroe. "One columnist wrote that I was cheap and vulgar in it," Marilyn said, "and that I would've looked better in a potato sack. So somebody in publicity asked, 'So O.K., why don't we put old Marilyn in a potato sack?'" Over four hundred newspapers across the country published at least one of the various poses in early 1952.

Although Marilyn's cheesecake pictures were considered very sexy, they were heavily censored by the studio, much to her dismay. "The Johnston office kills practically everything taken of me— and what the Johnston office passes the studio retouches. They spend a lot of time worrying about whether a girl has cleavage or not. It seems to me they ought to worry if she doesn't have any."

Another publicity gimmick: "Sexy blond starlet Marilyn Monroe returns to her alma mater, Van Nuys High School, and gives a few of the students pointers on attaining success in life."

OPPOSITE By the end of 1951 Marilyn was on the verge of major stardom. She appeared on the front page of *Stars and Stripes*, the serviceman's newspaper, every day for weeks—and when there weren't any new pictures available, the editors reprinted old ones. She was profiled in movie magazines as an orphan waif struggling to the top. One of the reasons Marilyn captured the imagination of so many men during this period was pictures like this. If you're good, you might find in your stocking this Christmas…

OPPOSITE Marilyn poses again for the publicity machine, checking the card file at the University of California library for a night class in which she enrolled. "She's very serious," the caption read, "about her course in 'Backgrounds in Literature.'"

On the set of *We're Not Married* with dialogue director Tony Jowitt, January 1952. The film was a series of stories of couples who discover their marriages are illegal. Marilyn played a wife who wins the Mrs. Mississippi contest, much to her husband's dismay. He welcomes the news that they're not married because she can no longer be Mrs. Mississippi. Of course, she immediately enters the Miss Mississippi pageant—which she wins as former husband and baby look on.

In April 1952 *Life* magazine featured a sexy Marilyn on its cover and billed her as "the talk of Hollywood." If she wasn't before, she surely was now. These rejected poses are as appealing as the photo used, and photographer Philippe Halsman later recalled that at this time "she was at the height of her sex appeal; and everything she did, every motion, was a mixture of conscious and unconscious appeal and challenge to the desire of men. …Though I have photographed hundreds of actresses, I have never seen one with a greater inferiority complex….She always had the feeling that she was not good enough, that she was unworthy; even her sex appeal stemmed from this. When she faced a man she didn't know, she felt safe and secure only when she knew the man desired her; so everything in her life was geared to provoke this feeling. Her talent in this respect was very great. I remember my experience in her tiny apartment with my assistant and the *Life* researcher. Each of us felt that if the other two would leave, something incredible would happen….She would try to seduce the camera as if it were a human being…. She knew that the camera lens was not just a glass eye but a symbol for the eyes of millions of men; so the camera stimulated her strongly. Because she had a great talent for directing the entire impact of her personality at the lens she was a remarkably gifted and exciting model."

On the set of *Monkey Business* with one of her co-stars, summer 1952. The others were Cary Grant, Ginger Rogers, and Charles Coburn. The film did little more than allow more people to experience Marilyn. As Paul V. Beckley of the New York *Herald Tribune* wrote, "Not having seen Miss Monroe before, I know now what that's all about, and I've no dissenting opinions to offer. She disproves more than adequately the efficacy of the old stage rule about not turning one's back to the audience."

OPPOSITE Marilyn's first starring role, and her most dramatic, was in Fox's *Don't Bother to Knock;* she played a psychotic baby-sitter. During filming in early 1952, the revelation that Marilyn had posed nude for a calendar five years earlier hit the newspapers. The studio front office first tried to squelch the story, then told Marilyn to deny it. Terrified that her highly promising career would be ruined, Marilyn sought advice and finally refused to lie. "I was broke and needed the money," she said. "I'm not ashamed of it. I've done nothing wrong." Her candor and the beauty of the calendar photo turned a potential public relations disaster into a swirl of sympathy and publicity for Monroe. By the time *Don't Bother to Knock* was released in the summer of 1952, Marilyn was indeed, as *Life* had called her, "the most talked-about actress in America." Her performance, however, got poor reviews; most critics felt she was out of her depth. The film was not a big hit; what money it did make, though, was attributed to Marilyn's rapidly burgeoning popularity.

The rumors are confirmed. Marilyn poses with baseball immortal Joe DiMaggio on the *Monkey Business* set—their first photo together. Joe had wanted to meet Marilyn ever since he saw that photo of her at bat, and a mutual friend arranged a blind date. "We almost didn't meet," Marilyn said. "I'd heard of Joe DiMaggio but I didn't know much about him. I've never followed baseball....I was very tired the night of the date and asked if I could get out of it. But I'd promised. I had visualized him as having slick black hair, wearing flashy sports clothes, with a New York line of patter....He had no line at all. No jokes. He was shy and reserved but, at the same time, rather warm and friendly. I noticed that he wasn't eating the food in front of him, that he was looking at me. Then the next thing I noticed was that I wasn't tired anymore. Joe asked me to have dinner with him the next night. I had dinner with him that night, the next night and every night until he had to leave for New York. I haven't dated anyone else."

On May 6, 1952, Monroe has her appendix removed and receives thousands of get-well greetings. Her doctor, preparing to operate, found a hand-written note Scotch-taped to her stomach: "Please take only what you *have* to. And please, please, no major scars."

A few days earlier, another Monroe revelation had made national news. Hollywood correspondent Erskine Johnson's newswire dispatch gave the details: "Marilyn Monroe—Hollywood's confessin' glamour doll who made recent headlines with the admission that she was a nude calendar cutie—confessed again today. Highly publicized by Hollywood press agents as an orphan waif who never knew her parents, Marilyn admitted she's the daughter of a one-time RKO studio film cutter, Gladys Baker, and said, 'I'm helping her and want to continue to help her when she needs me.' Said Hollywood's new glamour queen: 'My close friends know that my mother is alive. Unbeknown to me as a child, my mother spent many years in a state hospital. I haven't known my mother intimately, but since I've become grown and able to help her, I have contacted her.' The news that Marilyn's mother is alive and in Hollywood came as an eyebrow-lifting surprise."

Marilyn appears in court on June 25, 1952, to deny that she ever sent out letters soliciting sales of pornographic pictures of herself, or that she had ever posed for anything but *that* calendar. The letters and pictures were exposed as fakes, and two men were found guilty of misdemeanor charges in the scam.

OPPOSITE Marilyn plays a murderess on NBC radio's "Hollywood Star Playhouse," 1952.

Taking a break during the filming of *O'Henry's Full House*, another vignette film, in which she played a prostitute opposite Charles Laughton. Her part was very small; Fox was still often using her as little more than window dressing.

ABOVE As Rose Loomis, the amoral, unfaithful wife in *Niagara* (1953). It was Marilyn's juiciest part ever; her acting was quite credible, and she was now a bona fide movie star. Her costar, Joseph Cotten, was impressed: "Everything that girl does is sexy," he said. "A lot of people—the ones who haven't met Marilyn—will tell you it's all publicity. That's malarkey. They've tried to give a hundred other girls the same publicity buildup. It didn't take with them. This girl's really got it."

In *Niagara*, the camera lingers on Monroe's derriere during one long sequence in which she walks, as one wit put it, "horizontally." The walk created still another stir around Marilyn. Her associates were questioned intensely about *why* she undulated so when she walked. Emmeline Snively explained that MM was double-jointed. Sidney Skolsky answered that she had broken her ankle as a young girl and the walk resulted from her favoring the injured leg. "I don't know where they get these things," Marilyn said. "I've never been double-jointed. I've never had an accident. I walk the way I've always walked. I've walked this way since I was eleven or twelve."

Niagara was a big success, grossing $6 million—a hefty sum in 1953. Marilyn's reviews were good. Otis Guernsey wrote in the New York *Herald Tribune:* "Miss Monroe plays the kind of wife whose dress, in the words of the script, 'is cut so low you can see her knees.' The dress is red. The actress has very pretty knees, and under [Henry] Hathaway's direction she gives the kind of serpentine performance that makes the audience hate her while admiring her." *Time*'s critic said: "What lifts the film above the commonplace is its star, Marilyn Monroe."

OPPOSITE On a trip to New York in late August 1952 to promote *Monkey Business*, Marilyn mulls over questions during an interview at the Sherry Netherland Hotel. Asked about Joe, she replied, "We're just friends. He's a wonderful person." But the next day's news story would offer the opinion that they'd be married within thirty days.

Marilyn was fast becoming renowned for her "Monroeisms," *bons mots* which at first were thought to have been the invention of her press agents but which were genuinely her own. Hedda Hopper wrote: "She is fast supplanting Sam Goldwyn as a source of anecdotes." Some of her better quips:

Q. Did you have *anything* on when you posed for that calendar?

A: Yes. The radio.

Q: You're so pale. Why don't you get a tan?

A: I like to feel blond all over.

Q: Why don't you wear underwear?

A: I don't like to feel wrinkles.

In Atlantic City for the 1952 Miss America pageant, Marilyn was asked to pose with "the real Miss Americas," women in the Armed Services, as part of a "glamour" recruitment campaign. An enterprising photographer stood on a chair to capture the full measure of the Monroe cleavage. The photo wasn't given much press play because of the plenitude of beautiful women at the pageant; most papers were interested more in their state's entry. But an irate army information officer, aghast at the thought that the picture would give parents of potential recruits "a wrong impression of Army life," ordered that the picture be killed. Of course, it then received tremendous play, running seven columns wide in the Los Angeles *Herald and Express* and on front pages across the country. Marilyn was asked about the brouhaha, and in a story under the headline "Marilyn Wounded by Army Blushoff," she said, "I am very surprised and very hurt. I wasn't aware of any objectionable decolletage on my part. I'd noticed people looking at me all day, but I thought they were admiring my Grand Marshal's badge."

59

OPPOSITE Marilyn waves to the crowds along the streets of Atlantic City during a parade preceding the pageant. MM was the parade's Grand Marshal.

November 1952: Monroe does a guest stint on the Edgar Bergen–Charlie McCarthy radio program and announces that she and the precocious wooden celebrity are engaged to be married.

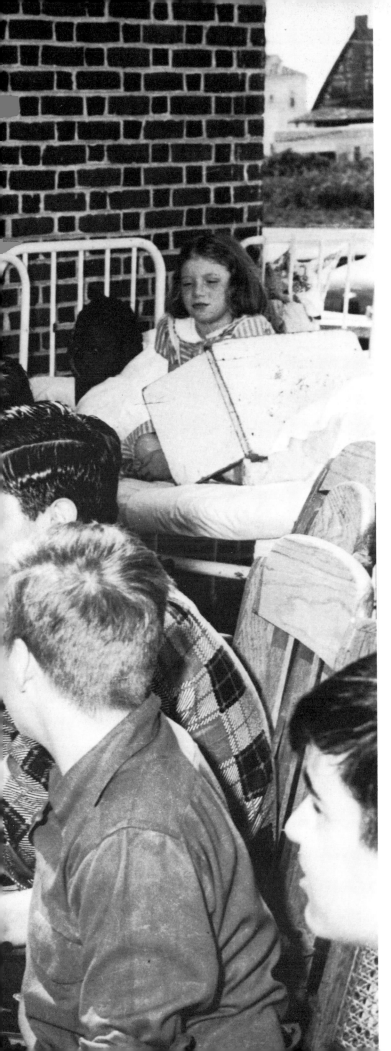

While on her trip East, Monroe made some young men very happy with an impromptu visit to a hospital.

Part Four

Phenomenon

1953-1955

Marilyn receives the *Redbook* Award in March of 1953 as the "Best Young Box Office Personality." With her are Leslie Caron, Dean Martin, *Redbook* editor Wade Nichols, and Jerry Lewis. By now she was receiving 25,000 fan letters a week.

OPPOSITE With Louella Parsons on the set of *Gentlemen Prefer Blondes*, MM's first extravagant, expensive musical, in 1953. Parsons and her fellow gossip columnist Hedda Hopper were instrumental in Marilyn's success. Parsons was of particular help; shortly before this she had chosen Marilyn as the No. 1 Movie Glamour Girl, a selection that received heavy newspaper coverage. "She had to be the winner," Parsons wrote. "It is Marilyn who is number one on all the GI polls of Hollywood favorites, and number one on exhibitors' polls of box office favorites. She is the number one cover girl of the year, and certainly number one in public interest wherever she goes."

"I just love finding new places to wear diamonds!"
Marilyn as Lorelei Lee, fortune hunter, and Jane
Russell as Dorothy Shaw, husband hunter, in *Gentlemen Prefer Blondes*. The press tried to build up a
feud between the two stars, but they developed a
strong friendship. Working with Marilyn, Jane
reported, was an interesting experience: "Marilyn
is a dreamy girl. She's the kind liable to show up
with one red shoe and one black shoe....I'd find
out when we'd take a break at eleven that she
hadn't had any breakfast and forgot she was
hungry until I reminded her. She once got her life
so balled up that the studio hired a full-time secre-
tary-maid for her. So Marilyn soon got the secretary as balled up as she was, and she ended up waiting on the secretary instead of vice-versa."

On the set with George Winslow, her young co-star. Later he would tell the story of seeing a woman who said good night to him every evening after work—a woman he didn't recognize. It was only later that he realized it was Marilyn—without costumes or makeup.

OPPOSITE Her big number: "Diamonds Are a Girl's Best Friend." She had to convince Darryl Zanuck she could sing by doing the number a cappella in his office. *Gentlemen Prefer Blondes* was a huge box office success, and Marilyn was now clearly the most potent box office force in Hollywood. Her reviews were good, although there were some critics who resisted being swept up in the country's "Monroe Mania." Otis Guernsey, however, summed up the popular reaction to MM: "Marilyn looks as though she would glow in the dark, and her version of the baby-faced blonde whose eyes open for diamonds and close for kisses is always as amusing as it is alluring."

In March 1953, Marilyn poses happily with her *Photoplay* Award as "Fastest Rising Star of 1952." Her pleasure wasn't to last long, however. Her dress—a costume from *Blondes* into which she had to be sewn—became the focal point of a storm of criticism. She had had her detractors before—those who thought her "cheap and vulgar"—but never before anyone as respected as Joan Crawford. The Oscar-winning actress, present at the award ceremony, was appalled when MM sauntered in. "It was like a burlesque show," Crawford told reporter Bob Thomas for a nationally syndicated story. "The audience yelled and shouted, and Jerry Lewis got up on the table and whistled. But those of us in the industry just shuddered…sex plays a tremendously important part in every person's life. People are interested in it, intrigued with it. But they don't like to see it flaunted in their faces…the publicity has gone too far. She is making the mistake of believing her publicity. She should be told that the public likes provocative feminine personalities, but it also likes to know that underneath it all, the actresses are ladies."

Marilyn was devastated by Crawford's attack, and the fact that Joe DiMaggio agreed made things all the worse. Marilyn went into seclusion for several days, then replied through Louella Parsons' influential column. "I think the thing that hit me hardest about Miss Crawford's story," Marilyn said, "is that it came from her. I've always admired her for being such a wonderful mother—for taking four children and giving them a fine home. Who, better than I, knows what it means to homeless little ones?"

Filming *How to Marry a Millionaire*, 1953. This pose was used to illustrate the wide-angle wonder of CinemaScope, the revolutionary new process that had been used previously only for the biblical epic *The Robe*.

OPPOSITE With *Millionaire* costar Lauren Bacall. At first Marilyn resisted playing the role of Pola, a hopelessly nearsighted lass who won't wear her glasses when men are around because, "men aren't attentive to girls who wear glasses." Monroe thought she would look terrible and that the public wouldn't like her that way. But the role actually won her new admirers; she displayed fine comic timing and a charming self-effacement. Nunnally Johnson, the film's writer and producer, said: "I believe that the first time anyone genuinely liked Marilyn for herself, in a picture, was in *Millionaire*. She herself diagnosed the reason for that very shrewdly, I think. She said that this was the only picture she'd been in in which she had a measure of modesty about her own attractiveness...she didn't think men would look at her twice, because she wore glasses; she blundered into walls and stumbled into things and she was most disarming....In her other pictures they've cast her as a somewhat arrogant sex trap, but when *Millionaire* was released, I heard people say, 'Why, I really like her!' in surprised tones."

Marilyn, Lauren, and the third *Millionaire* glamour doll, Betty Grable, pose with a visitor to the set. Bacall was rather cool toward Marilyn, but Grable treated her with kindness, despite the fact that Marilyn was said to be replacing Grable as Fox's blond sex symbol. Betty told Marilyn, "Honey, I've had it. Go get yours. It's your turn now."

In her autobiography, Bacall wrote: "Marilyn was frightened, insecure, trusted only her coach and was always late. During our scenes she'd look at my forehead instead of my eyes, and at the end of a take, look at her coach...if the headshake was no, she'd insist on another take. A scene often went to fifteen or more takes...not easy, often irritating. And yet I didn't dislike Marilyn. She had no meanness in her—no bitchery....There was something sad about her—wanting to reach out—afraid to trust—uncomfortable. She made no effort for others and yet she was nice. I think she did trust me and like me as much as she could anyone whose life must have seemed so secure, so *solved*."

Monroe and Russell put their handprints and sig-
natures in cement in the forecourt of Grauman's
Chinese Theater in Hollywood, 1953. It was a hal-
lowed Hollywood tradition and a sure sign of success. Marilyn's mother had taken her there twenty
years earlier to see the stars' hand- and footprints.
"I used to try and fit my hands and feet in the stars'
prints," she said. "The only ones that fit were
Rudolph Valentino's." Marilyn suggested that if
these "prints" were supposed to reflect your public
personality, Jane Russell should bend over into the
cement and she should sit in it. The idea was nixed,
as was her suggestion that a diamond be used to
dot her *i*. A rhinestone was put in place as a compromise; it was pried loose by a thief shortly
thereafter.

OPPOSITE   Q: "What do you wear to bed, Marilyn?"   A: "Chanel No. 5."

OPPOSITE With her drama coach, Natasha Lytess, in Canada during the filming of *River of No Return*, late 1953. The film was directed by Otto Preminger and costarred Robert Mitchum and Rory Calhoun. Marilyn relied so heavily on Natasha's coaching that Preminger began to hate them both. His autobiography's chapter on Marilyn is almost entirely a diatribe against Lytess. But Marilyn thought the woman vital to her goals. "You're wonderful, Marilyn," Lytess once told her; "I love you." Monroe replied, "Don't love me. *Teach* me."

Preminger and Monroe were constantly at odds. He found her totally exasperating in her tardiness, her reliance on Lytess, her vagueness. She thought him tyrannical, insensitive, mean. She sprained her ankle at one point and filming had to be done around her until she could get back to work. Shelley Winters, in her autobiography, says that her friend Marilyn faked the severity of the sprain in order to get Preminger to "go easy on her" and win sympathy. The ploy worked; Preminger was told by Fox brass to treat his star with more kindness and patience. Here Marilyn shows that nothing can detract from her appeal.

Joe DiMaggio pays Marilyn a visit after hearing of her sprain. He brought his own doctor with him to take a look at Marilyn's ankle. Joe's visit added fuel to the gossipy fires, and there was speculation that the couple were either engaged or already secretly wed. Marilyn denied the latter. "I wouldn't want to keep my marriage secret—there wouldn't be any reason to. Where could Joe and I marry, anyway, that the whole world wouldn't know about it?" But after almost two years of saying "Joe and I are just friends," Marilyn admitted, "I'm sure I'm in love with him. I know I like him better than any man I ever met." Asked how close they were, Marilyn smiled and said, "We haven't gotten around to baseball yet." Another time she revealed coyly, "Joe has great coordination."

The "storybook romance" added considerable interest to the already fascinating Monroe Story. She appeared on the covers of thirteen magazines *in a single month* in 1953—and almost every day the New York newspapers carried some item or photo about her, or her and Joe. New York, the center of world media, was enchanted by the love affair of "America's glamour queen" and "Joltin' Joe, the Yankee Clipper." It was a double-threat story, and whether the press created the intense national interest in it or simply reacted to the interest already there is a moot point. The country was enraptured.

River of No Return proved an unfortunate movie for Marilyn: it had a laughable script, garish costumes, and a tacky character for Monroe to play. She described it as "a Z cowboy movie in which the acting finishes third to the scenery and Cinema-Scope." She still, despite her superstardom, did not have any say in the roles she was to play, and she would soon rebel. But *River of No Return* did nothing to tarnish her glamorous image—Marilyn looked just as spectacular as the Canadian wilds.

OPPOSITE Marilyn and Jack Benny get together to prepare for her national television debut on his show, September 13, 1953. "Marilyn is probably the most important guest to appear on my show in a long time," Benny said, "and I'm highly flattered she's going to be on my program."

Monroe waits to make her entrance on the Benny show. Her appearance, during which Benny resists her passionate advances, prompted commentator Faye Emerson to write: "Let's face it, girls, here is the champ! She's here to stay for a long time. From the moment she ran into our camera until she slithered off with a long last glance that withered the men in our house, this little girl was in charge....She glistened from the top of her platinum head all the way down her famous torso...everything worked."

BELOW Wearing the same dress she wore on the Benny show, Marilyn attends the glittering premiere of *How to Marry a Millionaire*, November 1953. It was a consummate night for Marilyn—a huge crowd of fans roared her name as she alighted from a limousine amid exploding flashbulbs. The adulation was intoxicating, she told a companion. "I guess this is just about the happiest night of my life. Somehow it's like when I was a little girl and pretended wonderful things were happening to me. Now they are." The premiere was star-studded (here Lauren Bacall's husband, Humphrey Bogart, poses with Marilyn), but she was the center of attention. That night she was the biggest star in the world—and *Millionaire* went on to be a smashing box office success.

OPPOSITE At a Hollywood party, late 1953. Little Norma Jeane Baker had achieved her dream—she knew what it was like to be beautiful, famous, glamorous, and loved. But it wasn't all she had dreamed it would be. "It's funny," she said, "how success makes so many people hate you. I wish it wasn't that way. It would be wonderful to enjoy success without seeing envy in the eyes of those around you."

OPPOSITE "The Marriage of the Decade." January 14, 1954, Marilyn and Joe tie the knot in San Francisco. Marilyn promised to tell her friend, Fox publicist Harry Brand, when she was going to marry Joe. She did, and he let the word out. Reporters swarmed around the courthouse and the bedlam was so outrageous the judge forgot to kiss the bride. America was agog: the Los Angeles *Herald and Express* said: "It could only happen here in America, this storybook romance.... Both of them...had to fight their way to fame and fortune and to each other; one in a birthday suit, as a foundling and later as a calendar girl; the other in a ...baseball suit."

The couple traveled to Paso Robles and stayed one night at a motel. Joe, a TV addict, inquired whether the room had a television(!). The next day they left for a mountain hideaway fifty miles from Palm Springs. There was snow on the ground, and they were alone for two weeks. "There wasn't a television set in the cabin," Marilyn said. "Joe and I talked a lot. We really got to know each other."

Arriving in Japan for a honeymoon trip, MM tells the press that her stole is fox—"not the Twentieth Century kind." She had been suspended by the studio for refusing to do *The Girl in Pink Tights*, a film she thought unworthy of her. (She had *heard* it was unworthy of her—they wouldn't show her the script.) She also wanted more money—because of her seven-year pact, actors without her box office impact were making much more per picture than she. Fox was determined not to give in to her "unreasonable demands"—but now that she was Mrs. Joe D., what was a studio to do? It lifted the suspension.

Marilyn meets the boys who helped make her a star—and the results are explosive: 100,000 servicemen in Korea cheer, stomp, catcall, and incessantly snap cameras as Marilyn sings for them in the bitter cold. She almost caused a riot; several men were nearly trampled in the attempt to get as close to her as possible. She was as coy and sexy as she could get away with. Typical of her repartee: "You fellas are always whistling at sweater girls. Well, take away their sweaters and what have you got?"

At subsequent stops, Monroe wore a skimpy jacket as some protection against the chill—she was developing a bad cold and laryngitis. But she continued, and the Army later figured she'd done more for the soldiers' morale than anyone else could have. Back in Tokyo, she remembered the experience with a thrill. "It was so wonderful, Joe," she told her husband. "You never heard such cheering."

"Yes I have," he replied. "Don't let it go to your head. Just miss the ball once. You'll see they can boo as loud as they can cheer."

OPPOSITE Marilyn, now suffering from pneumonia, arrives back in the States with a protective Joe, who refused to allow her to be interviewed by the waiting newsmen.

Two weeks later, in March 1954, a nicely recovered Marilyn accepts her second *Photoplay* award, this time as "Best Actress" for *Gentlemen Prefer Blondes* and *How to Marry a Millionaire.* "This award means a lot to me," she said, "because it's for my *performance.*" With her is Alan Ladd.

OPPOSITE With Hedda Hopper, the other half of the gossipy dynamic duo who dominated Hollywood in the forties and fifties. Marilyn is in costume for her role in 1954's *There's No Business Like Show Business,* her first film after returning to the Twentieth Century-Fox fold. She accepted the part because Fox promised her the choicest comedy role then available, the "girl upstairs" in *The Seven Year Itch.*

Rehearsing the "There's No Business Like Show Business" number with her costars Johnnie Ray, Mitzi Gaynor, Dan Dailey, Ethel Merman, and Donald O'Connor. Monroe must have felt a film based on Irving Berlin's music and starring such talented performers would be preferable to *The Girl in Pink Tights*, but the choice was an unfortunate one. She played Donald O'Connor's love interest, and his youthful, fresh appearance made her seem, with her heavy makeup, artificial and "old enough to be his mother," as she put it.

Although she looks demure in this on-the-set candid, Marilyn's musical numbers turned out vulgar and garish, and her performance was surprisingly stiff after the comic flair she had displayed in previous films. There was much condemnation of one of her numbers in particular, "Heat Wave." The film itself contained little wit, style, or taste, and her embarrassment over the whole thing hardened her resolve not to let herself get talked into "Grade Z" movies anymore. After *There's No Business Like Show Business* her films, with one exception, would all be of memorable excellence.

OPPOSITE In New York for location shooting of *The Seven Year Itch*, in September 1954, Marilyn assumes an unusually somber mood. She was delighted to be making this film and grateful for the opportunity to star in Billy Wilder's version of George Axelrod's smash Broadway play, a proven vehicle with a well-written, witty female lead.

The celebrated "skirt-blowing scene," filmed on September 15, 1954. Marilyn stands over a New York subway grating, and the turbulence created by the train passing underneath (actually a huge electric fan) lifts her dress and millions of masculine spirits. The filming, witnessed by two thousand spectators, reporters, and photographers, caused traffic jams and lifted something else besides MM's skirt—Joe DiMaggio's temper. Infuriated by his wife's "public spectacle," he watched grim-faced and at one point muttered, "What the hell is going on here?" Director Wilder commented, "I shall never forget the look of death on Joe's face."

90

OPPOSITE The DiMaggios return to California amid rumors that their marriage is in trouble.

The "storybook marriage" comes to an end. On October 5, 1954, attorney Jerry Geisler escorts Marilyn out of the house she and Joe shared in Beverly Hills and a crowd of a hundred newspeople push forward. The marriage had lasted less than nine months. Marilyn, near collapse and unable to talk coherently, would only say "I'm sorry" whenever she was thrown a question. Geisler asked the press boys to lay off. "She's emotionally distraught. She and Joe couldn't get along. All the information you want will be brought out at the proper time."

Monroe reported to work on *The Seven Year Itch* later that day, but Billy Wilder sent her home. "She has a comedy part," he explained, "and she couldn't see much comedy in life today."

Three weeks later, a more composed Marilyn signs the divorce decree. The official reason for the breakup was listed as "incompatibility." Joe had wanted Marilyn to give up her career and be solely his wife. She couldn't do it. He, according to Marilyn, "didn't talk to me. He was cold. He was indifferent to me as a human being and an artist. He didn't want me to have friends of my own. He didn't want me to do my work. He watched television instead of talking to me." Later she added, "Joe distrusted everybody in Hollywood except his buddy Frank Sinatra. We just lived in two different worlds. He spent all day in front of the TV set watching some game or another. He went for days without even speaking to me. He's the moodiest man I ever met."

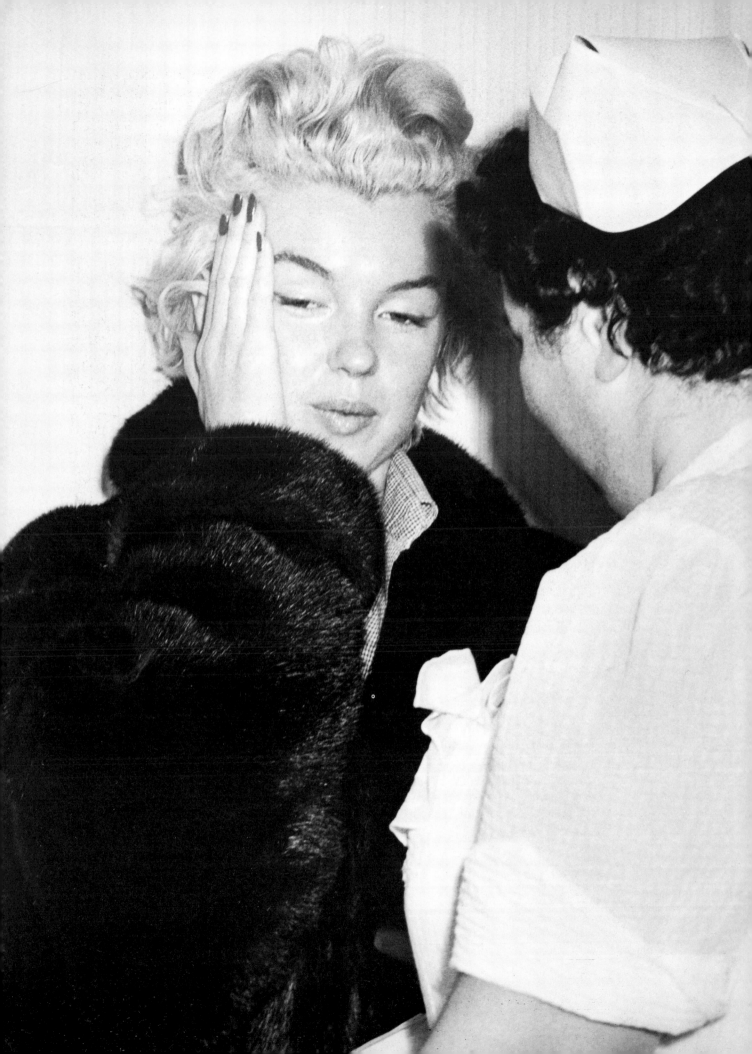

OPPOSITE After undergoing minor surgery in November 1954, Marilyn checks out of Cedars of Lebanon hospital and is appalled to discover photographers there to record the event. She had come to expect cameras everywhere she went publicly, but now she had to face a total lack of privacy—something which disturbed her greatly.

Bouncing back, Marilyn attends a performance by Ella Fitzgerald in Hollywood, escorted by columnist Sidney Skolsky, a friend. Throughout her life, Ella and Frank Sinatra would remain her two favorite vocalists.

OPPOSITE The unveiling of the "New Marilyn." January 7, 1955, in New York, she calls a press conference to announce that she and photographer Milton Greene had formed Marilyn Monroe Productions, Inc., "so I can play the better kind of roles I want to play. I didn't like a lot of my pictures. I'm tired of sex roles. I want to broaden my scope. I want to do dramatic parts." Asked if, as rumored, she wanted "to play *The Brothers Karamazov*," she replied, "I don't want to play the brothers. I want to play Grushenka. She's a girl." Then she added, "It's no temptation to me to do the same thing over and over. I want to keep growing as a person and as an actress...in Hollywood they never ask me my opinion. They just tell me what time to come to work."

Later that day, Monroe meets Dietrich as Milton Greene looks on. Of Greene, who was to take some of the loveliest pictures of her ever, Marilyn said, "I think he's very capable and very talented and very artistic, and a lot of other people will know it someday. You'll see. I feel deeply about him. I'm sincere about his genius. He's a genius."

Marilyn gives herself to charity. She also gave herself to Milton Berle, if Uncle Miltie's autobiography is to be believed—he claims they had an affair.

March 31, 1955: Marilyn rides a pink elephant at a Madison Square Garden extravaganza put on by showman Mike Todd to benefit victims of arthritis. Joe DiMaggio was in the audience; that and their several dates over the previous three months had reconciliation rumors swirling.

President Monroe and V.P. Greene outside the corporate offices of Marilyn Monroe Productions, Inc. It was Fox's insistence that she star in a "degrading" film, *How to Be Very, Very Popular*, that led to her latest walkout and the "New Monroe Doctrine"—as the press dubbed it—of independence. "I want to be an artist," she said. "Not a freak."

OPPOSITE The quintessential Marilyn with her favorite perfume.

A night at El Morocco with Truman Capote, May 1955. They understood each other, Capote says. In his essay on Monroe, "A Beautiful Child," Capote recalled Marilyn's asking him what his best sexual experience was. He asked her to answer first. "Joe's not bad," she replied. "He can hit home runs. If that's all it takes, we'd still be married. I still love him, though. He's genuine." Capote's assessment of Monroe? "I don't think she's an actress at all, not in any traditional sense. What she has—this presence, this luminosity, this flickering intelligence—could never surface on the stage. It's so fragile and subtle, it can only be caught by the camera…but anyone who thinks this girl is simply another Harlow or harlot or whatever is *mad*."

In April 1955, Edward R. Murrow's "Person to Person" visits Marilyn at the Milton Greenes', where she was living after moving to New York. Monroe, so witty and effervescent at press conferences, became terrified at the thought of millions of TV viewers watching her live. She froze on screen, requiring Mrs. Greene to answer several questions for her, and the responses MM did give were often halting and vague. Marilyn, it was said, came off like "a scared rabbit"—some viewers thought her in need of protection from the wicked studio, others felt Fox should "forget about Marilyn and sign up Amy Greene." In any event, Monroe's appearance was the highest-rated "Person to Person" ever.

OPPOSITE On June 1, 1955 (Marilyn's twenty-ninth birthday), Joe DiMaggio escorts his ex-wife to the premiere of *The Seven Year Itch*. His hope for a reconciliation led him to agree to appear at the film's opening, something he'd never done before. Earlier in the year, during a date in Boston, a reporter asked Joe if this was a reconciliation. He turned to Marilyn. "Is it, honey?" She replied, "No, no…just call it a visit." Hearing that, DiMaggio refused to answer any further questions.

A 3½-story-high Marilyn advertises the opening of *The Seven Year Itch* on New York's Times Square. The mammoth MM created the predictable chaos and controversy, not least with Monroe herself. She thought her face looked ugly in this picture, and she insisted that Fox put up another. They did, at considerable expense.

Marilyn's reviews for *The Seven Year Itch* were excellent; she proved herself a sensitive comedienne well able to handle the rare nuances Axelrod had written into this "dumb blonde" character. Monroe's acting was beginning to gain admiration, if not quite respect. Her desire for that respect prompted her decision to move to New York, where she could study acting at Lee Strasberg's fabled Actors Studio.

OPPOSITE At a New York party toward the end of the year, Marilyn dances with Marlon Brando. He had long been her acting idol, and he was, she said, "one of the most attractive men I've ever met." Gossips longed for a romance ("imagine what their *kids* would look like!"), but by this time Marilyn was secretly involved with someone else—Pulitzer Prize-winning playwright Arthur Miller, author of *Death of a Salesman*.

Part Five

The New Marilyn
1956-1957

Marilyn's new life included a love affair with Manhattan. She would often take walks along a nearly deserted Park Avenue in the early morning hours and marvel at the skyscrapers and the chill. "I love it here. I lived in California all my life; now I plan to stay here. The California climate is wonderful, but I love to see the seasons."

OPPOSITE At a New York press conference in February of 1956 to announce that the first Marilyn Monroe production will be *The Sleeping Prince*, costarring Monroe and Laurence Olivier, Marilyn steals the show from Sir Laurence when her shoulder strap breaks. Monroe reiterated her dramatic ambitions, and Olivier opined that Monroe was "a brilliant comedienne, which to me means she is also an extremely skilled actress." But the newsmen gave Marilyn an unusually hard time. Contemptuous of her desire to be taken seriously as an actress, they grilled her unmercifully, asking questions such as "How do you spell Grushenka?" and, in a tone suggesting that it was all a stunt, "How did it feel when the strap broke?" Hurt and angered by the hostility, Marilyn snapped, "How would you feel if something of yours broke in front of a whole room full of a lot of strangers?"—and walked out.

Monroe—with a new, more natural hair color—poses outside the Actors Studio. Her association with Lee Strasberg and his Method actors would teach Marilyn a great deal about her own potential as an actress. She listened intently in class, just one of dozens of students; when her turn came to perform a scene in class—from *Anna Christie*, along with Maureen Stapleton—the consensus among her discriminating peers was that it was a touching, surprisingly realistic portrayal. Strasberg—who along with his wife, Paula, would remain a Monroe mentor until her death—saw tremendous raw talent in Marilyn. He was in fact to say that the two greatest talents he had encountered at the Actors Studio were Marlon Brando and Marilyn Monroe. It was this kind of belief in her ability that led Monroe to the marvelous performances she was to give in four of her next five films.

Returning to Hollywood to play Cherie in Joshua Logan's film of William Inge's critically acclaimed Broadway play *Bus Stop*, February 1956. Monroe had made peace with Twentieth Century-Fox, and *Bus Stop* would be her first film in a seven-year, four-picture contract worth $8 million. She also received a retroactive $100,000 to make up for her having worked for $500 a week on some of her biggest Fox hits. Even more important to her ("I don't care about money. I just want to be wonderful"), the contract guaranteed her script and director approval. The Los Angeles press treated her more civilly than the New York group had. One of the reporters asked, "Marilyn, when we last saw you, you were wearing a low-cut gown. Now you're wearing a high-necked suit. Is this the 'new Marilyn'?" Monroe thought a moment, pursed her lips, and replied, "Well, I'm the same person—it's just a different suit."

OPPOSITE Marilyn as Cherie, the pathetic saloon singer starved for respect. Joshua Logan has said that when he was told Monroe would play her, his reaction was, "Oh, no—Marilyn Monroe can't bring off *Bus Stop*. She can't act." Now he says, "I could gargle with salt and vinegar even now as I say that, because I found her to be one of the greatest talents of all time."

Monroe's chalky makeup, right for Cherie but deglamorizing, caused consternation in the Fox front office. They wanted it changed, but she and Logan held out. "Marilyn's attitude toward her makeup and costumes was courageous," Logan said. "Incredible, really. Here you have a well-established star. She was willing to risk her position with a makeup many stars would have considered ugly. She wasn't afraid. She believed she was right in her analysis of the character, and she had the courage to commit herself to it completely."

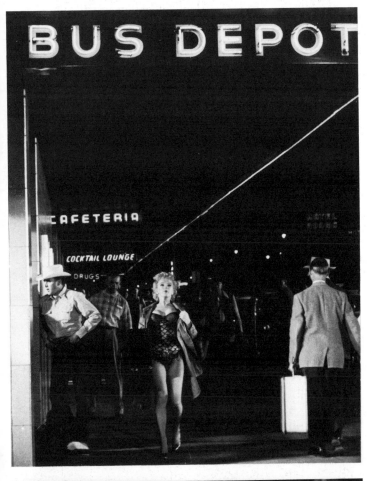

Logan didn't often experience Monroe's legendary difficulty, tardiness, or vagueness. "Marilyn was a totally satisfying professional during all the shooting in Phoenix," Logan says. But there was one instance of her lateness—while Logan was filming a scene in which Cherie flees her ardent cowboy suitor. Logan had only minutes of sunlight left and Marilyn was nowhere to be seen. Repeated efforts to get her had failed. With three minutes left, Logan ran to her dressing room, grabbed her by the arm, and ran with her back to the set. When she got there, flustered and out of breath, Logan yelled, "Action! Roll it! Roll it!" Marilyn's breathless fright in that scene was less a result of her Actors Studio training than her director's fury.

A rare glimpse of Marilyn's imperious side, which many of her costars and directors were to experience. Although Joshua Logan has only fond memories of working with Monroe, her costar Don Murray and she did not get along.

OPPOSITE Years after *Bus Stop* was completed, Joshua Logan would remain the director who most admired Marilyn; he later called her a combination of Chaplin and Garbo. "She was always the most beautiful person in the room, and certainly the most fun to talk to—warm, witty and with the enthusiasm of a child. Innocent, yes, but she was never ignorant, stupid or gross. She was in my opinion extremely bright, totally involved in her work. I think she was at some kind of peak in her emotional as well as intellectual life [then]. There are still those of us who remember that extraordinary performance, who know how badly she was judged by most of the world, including her so-called peers, how stupidly she was written about. Like Cherie, she was never able to feel what she longed for—respect."

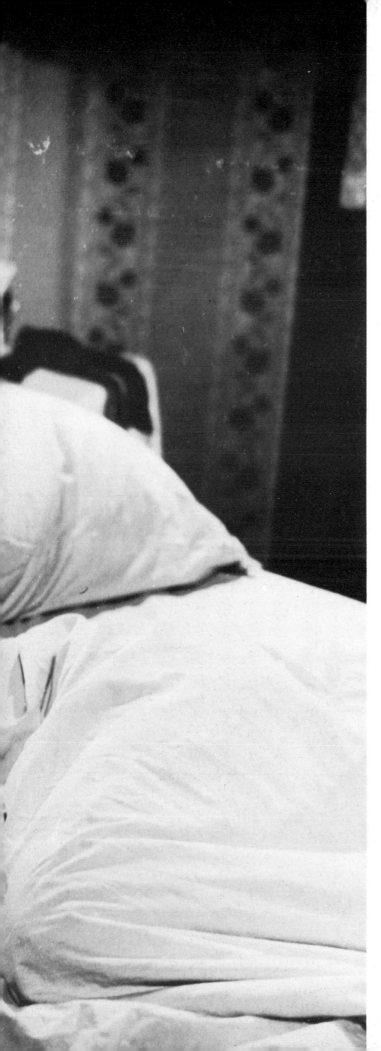

The release of *Bus Stop* resulted in high critical praise for Marilyn as "an artist, not a freak." Clearly, what she had learned at the Actors Studio helped her plumb greater acting depths than she had ever been able to before. Bosley Crowther began his New York *Times* review on August 1, 1956: "Hold onto your chairs, everybody, and get set for a rattling surprise. Marilyn Monroe has finally proved herself an actress in *Bus Stop*...she and the picture are swell!"

Arthur Knight wrote in *Saturday Review:* "In *Bus Stop* Marilyn Monroe effectively dispels once and for all the notion that she is merely a glamour personality, a shapely body with tremulous lips and come-hither blue eyes....For Miss Monroe has accomplished what is unquestionably the most difficult feat for any film personality. She has submerged herself so completely in the role of Inge's Hollywood-happy 'chantoosie' from the Ozarks that one searches in vain for glimpses of the former calendar girl. It is far more than simply mastering and maintaining a ludicrous accent and intonation throughout the picture; the character itself is rich and complex...there is pathos, humor and a desperate pride about the girl, and Miss Monroe brings all of this to life."

Despite reviews like this, Hollywood refused to acknowledge that Monroe was capable of a great performance. Although many observers felt she deserved an Oscar for her work, she wasn't even nominated—a slap in the face she would recall with hurt for years afterward.

OPPOSITE On June 21, 1956, back in New York, Marilyn is cornered outside her apartment by newsmen who had camped out to get the scoop on Monroe's impending marriage to Arthur Miller, the subject of almost daily speculation in the press. "Leave me alone, fellas," MM pleaded. "I look a mess." The photographers didn't leave her alone, however, and the exclusive photos of Monroe *sans* makeup went out over the nation's wire services.

Later the same day, Marilyn—this time ready for the cameras—talks to the press in the lobby of her apartment building and tells them that she and Miller plan to wed "before July 13." What kind of wedding? "Any kind." What is the secret of Miller's appeal? "Everything. Haven't you seen him?" How many children? "I'm not married yet!"

Marilyn poses joyfully with her husband-to-be and his parents, Isadore and Augusta Miller, at Miller's hideaway in Roxbury, Connecticut, on June 30, 1956. She immediately called her in-laws "Mom" and "Dad." The Miller family embraced Marilyn, and it brought her a tranquillity she had not known for years. "Until recently," Miller said, "I took my family for granted. But Marilyn never had one, and she made me appreciate what that means. When you see how much a family matters to her and you understand the depth of that feeling, you'd have to be an ox not to respond."

The wedding of "the egghead and the hourglass" takes place, July 1, 1956. They had been secretly married the day before in a civil ceremony, but this time a rabbi performed the rites for the Jewish Miller and his veiled, recently converted wife. The "unlikeliest love match ever" was official.

Marilyn took to her new life with verve. She learned to make matzo balls and her own bread and noodles. For Miller, Marilyn had "tremendous native feeling. She has more guts than a slaughter-house. Being with her, people want not to die. She's all woman, the most womanly woman in the world." "We're so congenial," Marilyn purred. "This is the first time I think I've been really in love. Arthur is a serious man, but he has a wonderful sense of humor. We laugh and joke a lot. I'm mad about him."

OPPOSITE Less than two weeks after their wedding, the Millers flew to London. Laurence Olivier and wife Vivien Leigh greet them at Parkside House, where they stayed during the visit. Marilyn created chaos among the normally staid British press. After photographers nearly trampled each other at a press conference to get close-ups of La Monroe, Lady Olivier asked her, "Are all your conferences like this?" "Well," she replied, "this is a little quieter than some of them." The London *Evening News* gushed, "She's here. She walks. She talks. She really is as luscious as strawberries and cream." But some members of the British press gave her as hard a time about her pretensions to great art as their American counterparts, asking her questions about Beethoven and intellectualism that she embarrassingly couldn't answer. But she won the day when she responded to the query "What inspired you to study acting?" She quipped, "Seeing my own pictures!"

The Millers, desirous of privacy to the point of antagonizing the cream of British society, go out for a bike ride in a park near their cottage, August 13. When someone commented that Marilyn looked "wobbly" on a bike, Miller said, "She's a lot better than I am."

OPPOSITE To Marilyn, Arthur Miller embodied a number of things extremely important to her. Her marriage to him, she felt, brought her the respectability she craved; that such a brilliant intellectual loved her proved that she was a worthwhile, intelligent person. Physically, he reminded her of one of her heroes, Abraham Lincoln; and that he was something of a surrogate father can be surmised from the fact that her nickname for him was "Popsie." This photo makes Marilyn's adoration of Miller quite apparent.

Marilyn—and her gown—stole the spotlight from her husband's play as they attended the opening of *A View from the Bridge* at London's Comedy Theatre, October 12. Miller responded to criticism that suggested Monroe should be more circumspect in her attire. "Why should someone like Marilyn pretend to be dressing like somebody's old aunt?"

OPPOSITE Marilyn waves to the crowd as she enters the Empire Theatre, London, for a Royal Command Film Performance...

...after which she is presented to Queen Elizabeth, October 29. The two Queens of their respective domains exchanged the usual pleasantries, but film clips of the meeting show Her Majesty running her eyes quite interestedly up and down the length of Marilyn's tight, revealing gown before extending her hand in greeting. Flanking Monroe are Victor Mature and Anthony Quayle.

Monroe is attended to during filming of *The Prince and the Showgirl*, the new title for *The Sleeping Prince*. The filming was not a pleasant experience for anyone involved. Marilyn was extremely insecure about working with someone of Laurence Olivier's stature—and her insecurity always manifested itself in illness, tardiness, inability to remember her lines, and temperament. Things weren't helped by Olivier's direction; he was said to want Marilyn to play the role the way Vivien Leigh had on the London stage, and he was completely unsympathetic to her rather unique methods of "getting into a character." At one point he told his star, "Okay, Marilyn—be sexy." She was so upset she didn't come out of her dressing room the rest of the day. She took to calling him sarcastically "Mr. Sir."

As tensions increased on the set, Marilyn became ill, holding up production and making the situation worse. The only thing that kept everyone from total despair was viewing the daily rushes, in which Marilyn was more incandescent than ever. As so often in the past, Marilyn's magic was enough to make one forgive her anything.

OPPOSITE Her beauty in *The Prince and the Showgirl* was extraordinary, even by Monroe standards. Her makeup was relatively natural, as were her hair color and speaking voice. Costar Dame Sybil Thorndike marveled, "She has an innocence which is so extraordinary; whatever she plays, however brazen a hussy, it always comes out as an innocent girl. I remember Sir Laurence saying one day during the filming: 'Look at that face—she could be five years old!'"

The adversaries play a love scene. At the end of filming, Marilyn apologized in front of the entire company for being "so beastly": "I hope you will all forgive me. It wasn't my fault. I've been very, very sick all through the picture. Please—please don't hold it against me."

La Monroe looks demure—and healthy—back in New York as she does a rare radio broadcast from the Waldorf-Astoria Hotel, December 18, 1956. Fans of trivia take note: this is the only time MM would wear her hair wave on the left side of her forehead.

OPPOSITE Marilyn meets reporters in Washington, D.C., on May 23, 1957, as Arthur Miller's contempt of Congress trial comes to an end. Questioned by the House Un-American Activities Committee, Miller had refused to name other writers with whom he had attended a 1947 Communist Party meeting. Miller stated that it was a harmless flirtation—"I supported causes that I would not support now." He had also agreed the year before to sign an anti-Communist oath in order to obtain a passport to accompany Marilyn to England. But he would not implicate anyone else in what many Americans considered a "witch-hunt": "I could not use the name of another person. I wouldn't make it tougher on the life of any other writer."

Marilyn told newsmen that she was "confident" her husband would be acquitted and that she had come to Washington "because I feel a woman's place is with her husband." A week later, Miller was convicted on two counts of contempt, each with a maximum sentence of $1,000 and one year in jail. Miller received a thirty-day suspended sentence and a $500 fine. He vowed to appeal the conviction.

February 1957: Marilyn tries to dodge pursuing photographers as she walks her dog, Hugo, outside her New York apartment. Shortly afterward she bought out Milton Greene's share of Marilyn Monroe Productions, saying, "My company was not set up merely to parcel out 49.6 percent of all my earnings to Mr. Greene for seven years." A strain had developed between Marilyn and Greene when she married Arthur Miller, who took over many of the protective functions Greene once performed for Monroe. Greene accepted a relative pittance for his share of the company. "My interest in Marilyn's career," he said, "was not for gain. She needed me at the time, and I put at her complete disposal whatever abilities I possessed."

Marilyn sips along with William, a 3½-year-old beneficiary of the free Milk Fund for babies. The premiere of *The Prince and the Showgirl*, scheduled for later that day, was for the benefit of the Milk Fund. Questioned about the truth of rumors that she was pregnant, Marilyn would only say, "No comment."

OPPOSITE Mr. and Mrs. Miller attend the opening of *The Prince and the Showgirl* at New York's Radio City Music Hall, June 13, 1957. The film, panned by a number of critics, contains one of Marilyn's best performances. Archer Winsten of the New York *Post* wrote: "As for Marilyn Monroe, she has never seemed more in command of herself as person and as comedienne. She manages to make her laughs without sacrificing the real Marilyn to play acting. This, of course, is something one can expect from great, talented, practiced performers. It comes as a pleasant surprise from Marilyn Monroe, who has been half-actress, half-sensation."

The performance would garner her great praise and several acting awards from outside the United States, but once again she would be denied an Oscar nomination.

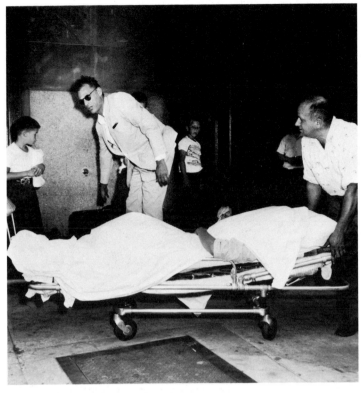

OPPOSITE On July 2, 1957, a pregnant Marilyn arrives two hours late to help break ground for the Time-Life Building near Rockefeller Center—fifteen hundred fans, twenty policemen, forty photographers, and Laurance Rockefeller waited patiently.

August 1, 1957: Marilyn suffers the first of three tragic miscarriages. After a high-speed four-hour ambulance ride from Amagansett, Long Island, she is wheeled into New York's Doctors Hospital, her face covered to protect her from the constantly popping flashbulbs. The baby was lost because of a rare complication: the fetus developed in her Fallopian tube rather than descending into the womb. Marilyn's inability to have children would haunt her the rest of her life.

Bravely facing the cameras again upon her release from the hospital on August 8, Marilyn gives the photographer a big smile. The Millers went back to their Amagansett home so that Marilyn could rest and recuperate; she would make no further public appearances for the rest of the year.

Part Six

Acclaim

1958-1959

January 28, 1958: Marilyn is kissed by the March of Dimes poster twins, Lindy and Sandy Sue Solomon, at a March of Dimes Fashion Show at New York's Waldorf-Astoria Hotel. Marilyn donated considerable time to charities involving children.

OPPOSITE In her Fifty-seventh Street apartment, MM models the new "sack" fashion, all the rage that season. "A sack allows you to move," Marilyn said. "And it moves with you. And movement is— well, movement is good."

April 25: producer Walter Mirisch and Marilyn discuss the script of *Some Like It Hot*, her next film, to be directed by Billy Wilder, the first director to agree to work with Marilyn a second time since she became a major star.

Marilyn and costar Tony Curtis at a cocktail party celebrating the impending start of *Some Like It Hot* filming. Later, the two would be considerably less cordial.

OPPOSITE Marilyn attends the Hollywood premiere of the film version of Lerner and Loewe's *Gigi* at the Paramount Theater.

August 8: Marilyn reacts joyfully to a phone call from Arthur Miller informing her that a U. S. Court of Appeals has reversed his contempt of Congress conviction. Miller said he hoped the court's decision would help "eliminate the excesses of Congressional Committees, particularly toward stopping the inhuman practice of making witnesses inform on long-past friends and acquaintances." Marilyn told the press, "I am very happy for my husband, but I am even happier for truth and justice that does exist in our country."

BELOW   As Sugar Kane in *Some Like It Hot.*

OPPOSITE   SUGAR: "My seams straight?" DAPHNE: "I'll say!" Tony Curtis and Jack Lemmon as musicians on the lam who join an all-girl band, only to run into Miss Kane, née Kowalcyck. DAPHNE: "Boy, would I like to borrow a cup of that sugar!"

When Monroe first learned that *Some Like It Hot* would be filmed in black and white, she balked. All her contracts stated that her films must be made in color. But Wilder showed her color tests of Lemmon and Curtis, and their heavy makeup had a sickly green tint on film. Marilyn relented.

OPPOSITE After a relatively pleasant experience with Marilyn during *The Seven Year Itch*, Billy Wilder was shocked to discover her extraordinarily vague, tardy, and temperamental. She would sometimes be ready for work at 4 P.M. after a 9 A.M. call. When she did show up, she would often forget or flub her lines. For one scene, she had to enter a room and say, "Where's the bourbon?" while looking through dresser drawers. She couldn't do it. Even when Wilder taped the words inside the drawers, for take after take she was unable to get the line right.

Monroe's need for retakes sent Tony Curtis into a fury. She would get better and brighter as she worked and warmed up, while Curtis would get tired and begin to sag. Curtis knew that Wilder had to choose Marilyn's best takes over his, and it galled him. Watching him make love to Marilyn on film during a screening, someone said to Curtis, "You look like you enjoyed kissing her, Tony." Curtis, a Jew, snorted and said, "Kissing her is like kissing Hitler!"

Arthur Miller visits his wife on location at Corona del Mar, California, September 10, 1958. Marilyn was pregnant, which made it all the more difficult for her to face the cameras each day. Miller's visits cheered her, but he was unable to help Billy Wilder get her to the set on time or help her remember her lines.

Between takes, Marilyn rests in the contraption designed to prevent her dress from wrinkling. With her is Paula Strasberg. Designer Orry-Kelly won an Oscar for this and Marilyn's other costumes in the film.

OPPOSITE Monroe films a scene of *Some Like It Hot* which required her to run again and again until Wilder was happy with the take. The strenuous activity caused her once again to lose a baby.

Marilyn and Arthur return to New York in December 1958, after her hospitalization. Miller soon found himself embroiled in a telegram war with Wilder over disparaging remarks the director had made about Monroe's unprofessionalism. Miller fired off a salvo reminding Wilder that he had been informed that, because of Marilyn's pregnancy, she could not work a full day, and stating that her efforts to do as much as possible caused her miscarriage. "Now that the hit for which she is so largely responsible is in your hands and its income to you assured, this attack upon her is contemptible. You are an unjust man and a cruel one. My only solace is that, despite you, her beauty and her humanity shine through as they always have."

Wilder replied: "Of course I am deeply sorry that she lost her baby. But I must reject the implication that overwork or inconsiderate treatment by me or anyone else associated with the production was in any way responsible for it. The fact is that the company pampered her, coddled her and acceded to all of her whims. The only one who showed any lack of consideration was Marilyn, in her treatment of her co-stars and her co-workers. Right from the first day, before there was any hint of pregnancy, her chronic tardiness and unpreparedness cost us eighteen shooting days, hundreds of thousands of dollars and countless heartaches."

Monroe receives the French equivalent of the Oscar for her performance in *The Prince and the Showgirl*, March 1959.

OPPOSITE MM in Chicago for that city's *Some Like It Hot* world premiere. Her incandescence has been explained as a result of her alabaster skin and platinum hair, but her masseur Ralph Roberts said it was more than that. "The skin layer right under the surface is moist and deep, like no other woman's. In the dark, her skin could light up a room."

At the New York premiere of *Some Like It Hot* in April, Marilyn looks like cotton candy that would glow in the dark. The film was a huge success, Monroe's biggest moneymaker, and was critically acclaimed as well. Her performance, for the fourth time in a row, was superb, and she was acknowledged by most critics as one of America's finest comediennes. The film has remained an American comedy classic, to which Monroe's contributions are clearly vital.

Her husband helps Marilyn out of a New York hospital on June 26 after she has undergone corrective surgery designed to allow her to bear children.

OPPOSITE More acclaim for her performance in *The Prince and the Showgirl*. Italy awards Marilyn its David di Donatello Prize, its version of the Oscar, as "Best Foreign Actress of 1958."

The Millers try to retain some privacy as they attend a performance of *Macbeth* in Boston, August 15, 1959.

OPPOSITE Monroe listens demurely at a Hollywood dinner in honor of visiting Soviet Premier Nikita Khrushchev, September 1959. She arrived on time, prompting Billy Wilder to quip, "Now I know who should direct all her pictures—Khrushchev!" Said Marilyn to her maid, Lena Pepitone, "I could tell Khrushchev liked me. He smiled more when he was introduced to me than for anybody else at the whole banquet. He squeezed my hand so long and hard I thought he would break it. I guess it was better than having to kiss him, though."

Part Seven

Decline

1960-1962

The Millers meet the Montands. A January 1960
Hollywood party introduced Marilyn's latest lead-
ing man, French actor-singer Yves Montand, and
his actress wife, Simone Signoret, to the press.
Marilyn and Yves were to costar in *Let's Make Love*,
Monroe's first film for Twentieth Century-Fox in
four years.

MM wins the Golden Globe Award as "Best Actress in a Comedy" for *Some Like It Hot*, March 8, 1960. She was again not nominated for an Oscar.

Marilyn is attended to while filming Let's Make Love, January 1960.

OPPOSITE "My Heart Belongs to Daddy," Marilyn's big production number in *Let's Make Love*, would prove to be one of the few bright spots in the film and the point at which she looked her loveliest. Monroe had been rather *zaftig* for several years. Once a reporter, irate at being kept waiting, asked her cattily, "Gained a little weight, haven't you, dearie?" She replied, "My husband likes me plump."

Marilyn seems serene on the set. But a fellow actor found a notebook of hers in which she had written: "What am I afraid of? Why am I so afraid? Do I think I can't act? I know I can act but I am afraid. I am afraid and I should not be and I must not be. Fuck!"

OPPOSITE Monroe listens intently to George Cukor's direction. Yves Montand told a reporter during filming, "Marilyn is a girl with a great many fears. She needs understanding, someone to calm her fears."

Marilyn looks on as one of the film's guest stars, Gene Kelly, teaches Montand a few dance steps. *Let's Make Love* turned out to be one of Marilyn's least effective films; the plot was labored and witless, and Monroe's characterization of showgirl Amanda Dell swung widely between naive and neurotic. For the most part her costumes were unflattering, and she often looked drawn and tired. It was the first film in which the traumas of Marilyn's personal life showed on her person on screen. The film was not a hit at the box office.

OPPOSITE With both their spouses out of town, Marilyn and Yves attend a preview of *The Apartment* in Hollywood. By now industry insiders knew they were having an affair. Monroe's marriage to Arthur Miller had been slowly coming apart for a variety of reasons, including his inability to handle her neuroses and her loss of respect for him as a result. She let herself get caught up in an infatuation for Montand and told a reporter, "Next to my husband and along with Marlon Brando, Yves Montand is the most attractive man I've ever met." Her first reaction upon seeing him, according to her maid, Lena Pepitone, was, "Doesn't he look like Joe?! I love his voice. He's so sexy! Wow!"

For Montand's part, his affair with Marilyn was a meaningless fling; he certainly had no intention of letting it break up his marriage. He told Hedda Hopper, "I think Marilyn is an enchanting child. ...She's a simple girl without any guile. Perhaps I was too tender and thought that maybe she was as sophisticated as some of the other ladies I have known. I've never known anyone quite like Marilyn Monroe. She is known throughout the world, but she is still a child."

Marilyn, needless to say, was mortified—and the situation did not help her shaky marriage at all.

ABOVE July 1960: Marilyn and Clark Gable at a party to celebrate the start of filming on *The Misfits*, a film written by Arthur Miller expressly for Marilyn and directed by John Huston. Gable was another of Monroe's girlhood idols and a man she often fantasized was her real father.

Marilyn with Thelma Ritter in the opening scene of *The Misfits*. She played Roslyn Tabor, a vague, neurotic, highly sexual woman with a deep melancholy, a love for animals, and a longing for her mother. The character, especially since it was written by Miller, hit a little too close to home; it was an extremely difficult role for Marilyn to play.

Filming *The Misfits*, Marilyn was under the greatest strain of her life. Shattered by the impending failure of a marriage that she thought would bring her lifelong love, security, and respectability, her miscarriages, and Yves Montand's rejection of her, she was barely able to function in the 100-degree heat of the Nevada desert. By now she had begun to drink heavily and to rely on various pills. "She took so many pills to help her sleep at night," John Huston later said, "that she had to take other pills to get her going in the morning. And that ravaged the girl."

She and Miller barely spoke; she often never showed up on the set, and when she did she was unable to perform. She drove Clark Gable to distraction, a fact that further upset her. Gable said as filming ended, "What the hell is that girl's problem? Goddamn it, I like her, but she's so damn unprofessional. I damn near went nuts up there in Reno waiting for her to show. Christ, she didn't show up until after lunch some days, and then she would blow take after take....I know she's heavy into booze and pills. Huston told me that. I think there's something wrong with the marriage. Too bad. I like Arthur, but that marriage ain't long for this world. Christ, I'm glad this picture's finished. She damn near gave me a heart attack."

BELOW The situation with Marilyn got so bad that John Huston was finally forced to close down production and send her to a Los Angeles hospital to get her off the alcohol and pills and allow her to rest. Two weeks later, September 5, 1960, Miller brought her back and she resumed filming.

OPPOSITE The first day back on the set, Marilyn gives the film one of its most charming moments. Her childlike glow regained, she leans across the breakfast table and asks Gable, "You like me, hunh?"

But the strains once again got to Marilyn; the entire *Misfits* filming was one of the most grueling in Hollywood history. It was chronicled in a book, *The Making of "The Misfits,"* and became the most expensive black-and-white picture made to that date.

The last day of filming, November 5, 1960, Gable hugs Monroe, both of them overjoyed that this excruciating ordeal is over. The next day Gable suffered a massive heart attack. Ten days later he died.

Soon after she completed *The Misfits*, Marilyn's life came apart. On November 11 she announced that her marriage to Arthur Miller was over, and ran the gauntlet of the press as she left her apartment. "Miller Walks Out on Marilyn," the New York *Daily News* headline screamed. With Gable's death four days later, Marilyn was at a low point in her life. After reading a gossip column item suggesting that Kay Gable blamed Marilyn for her husband's death, Marilyn came close to jumping out of her New York apartment window. She would put up a brave public front after that, but things only got worse.

January 31, 1961: costar Montgomery Clift escorts Marilyn to a New York preview of *The Misfits*. Marilyn's performance was praised by many critics; it was a complete departure from anything she had done before, and it presented a touching look at a sensitive, unhappy woman. The film was not a hit at the box office, but many film scholars regard it as one of the finest American films ever made.

OPPOSITE Marilyn is released from the Columbia Presbyterian Medical Center on March 5, 1961. It was at first announced that she had been hospitalized for "a rest," but press reports speculated it was worse than that ("Hint Marilyn May Be 'Greatly Disturbed' "). It was only years later that the full truth emerged: the recent events of her life and her growing dependence on drugs and alcohol had led her psychiatrist to admit her to the Payne Whitney Psychiatric Clinic in New York. There Marilyn found iron doors slamming behind her and bars on her windows. "What kind of place is this?" she screamed. "What are you doing to me?" With her grandparents, uncle, and mother all having been committed, Marilyn was terrified that she, too, would go insane. At Payne Whitney her fears were justified: there was a doorless toilet in her room and a glass pane on her door through which passing nurses could check on her. She degenerated into hysterics within two days.

She was allowed one call and phoned Joe DiMaggio in Florida. He came to New York immediately and used his considerable influence to have Marilyn released. He took her to Columbia Presbyterian, where she had a private room without bars. After three weeks of withdrawal from pills, Marilyn was released. Reporters crushed around her as usual, asking her to comment on Elizabeth Taylor's near-fatal illness. When she got home, she told Lena Pepitone, "They were going to put me in a straitjacket! Thank God for Joe. Thank God!"

More heartache: Marilyn attends the funeral of Arthur Miller's mother on March 8. With her is her secretary, May Reis.

OPPOSITE The harrowing year and a half Marilyn had been through shows clearly on her face as she attends a benefit for the Actors Studio at New York's Roseland Dance City on March 13, 1961.

"Thank God for Joe." Attempting to get her life back together, Marilyn vacations in Florida, where Joe DiMaggio has joined the New York Yankees for their spring training, March 1961. The trip was highly therapeutic for her. At one point, when "caught" leaving a motel by a photographer, Marilyn and Joe look extremely uncomfortable.

OPPOSITE Marilyn watches a Yankee batting practice.

Back in New York in April, Marilyn and Joe watch a game at Yankee Stadium. By now speculation about a remarriage was rampant in the press, but they would only say, "No comment."

OPPOSITE Looking serene and lovely, Marilyn attends the May 1961 christening of John Clark Gable, born months after his father's death. Marilyn was overjoyed at the invitation: it suggested that Kay Gable did not, after all, blame Monroe for Clark's death.

OPPOSITE Hospitalized again on June 29 for removal of her gallbladder, Monroe looks radiant as she is wheeled out of New York's Polyclinic Hospital to a waiting ambulance on July 11…

…but before long the huge crowd that had gathered to catch a glimpse of her became unruly. She was roughed up and very nearly injured in the melee.

Recuperating in California, Marilyn made very few public appearances during the rest of 1961.

OPPOSITE February 1962: Marilyn attends a performance of *Macbeth* in New York with Lee and Paula Strasberg.

Joe and Marilyn kiss good-bye after another Monroe visit to Florida, February 21, 1962. Marilyn said, "I loved being here," and when asked if she and Joe were on the road to a reconciliation, she replied, "I don't know what you mean. We're very good friends. There's nothing to reconcile." The press reports on Marilyn and Joe were accompanied by news of Arthur Miller's remarriage, to Inge Morath, a photographer he had met on the set of *The Misfits*.

At a February 26 press conference in Mexico, where she went to buy furnishings for her new Mexican-style home in Brentwood, near Los Angeles. Joe helped her with the house's purchase, and it was said he planned to buy the house next door in order to be near her.

Considering adopting a child, Marilyn visits an orphanage in Mexico. She never went through with the adoption plan, but she donated $1,000 to a local children's welfare institute that gave breakfasts to needy youngsters. "I know what it means to go without breakfast," she said.

Marilyn arrives at the Golden Globe Awards in Hollywood, March 1962.

OPPOSITE Rock Hudson and Steve Allen look on as Marilyn accepts a Golden Globe as the world's most popular star.

OPPOSITE With Dean Martin, her costar in *Something's Got to Give*, a comedy about a wife who returns from seven years on a desert island to discover her husband has remarried. It was a remake of the 1940 Cary Grant–Irene Dunne film *My Favorite Wife*.

The famous nude swimming sequence. Marilyn was so proud of the new slim figure her gallbladder surgery created that she shed the flesh-colored bathing suit she was wearing for the scene and agreed to pose *au naturel* for two photographers. The photos of a nude Marilyn sitting poolside were published throughout the world.

Amid rumors that Twentieth Century-Fox officials were considering replacing her in *Something's Got to Give* because of her repeated absences from the set, Marilyn flew to New York to sing at President Kennedy's forty-fifth birthday celebration in Madison Square Garden. Here she rehearses her performance.

May 19, 1962: Monroe's sexy, breathy rendition of "Happy Birthday" led President Kennedy to quip, "I can now retire from politics after having had 'Happy Birthday' sung to me in such a sweet, wholesome way."

OPPOSITE For many Monroe fans, this night represented the epitome of Marilyn's larger-than-life glamour. "I was honored when they asked me to appear at the President's birthday rally," Marilyn told *Life*. "There was like a hush over the whole place when I came on to sing 'Happy Birthday'—like if I had been wearing a slip I would have thought it was showing or something. I thought, Oh, my gosh, what if no sound comes out!"

186

OPPOSITE Back in Hollywood, Marilyn films a scene with costar Wally Cox. When she urges him to have lunch with her, he tells her he always brings his lunch with him and eats in. "I'd be ever so grateful if you'd take it out," she purrs.

ABOVE Monroe is directed by George Cukor. According to Nunnally Johnson, who wrote the screenplay of *How to Marry a Millionaire* and who had worked with Marilyn on a version of *Something's Got to Give* with which she was quite happy, Marilyn's chronic illness and frequent failures to report to work were a result of her fears and misgivings about George Cukor. He was not happy with the script and made changes, with many of which Marilyn disagreed. She felt frustrated and helpless and was afraid that a repeat of the *Let's Make Love* fiasco would ensue. Marilyn had had two box office flops in a row, and she had not had a

film in release in over eighteen months. This was to be her comeback picture, and if it failed, her career, she felt, might well be over.

As so often in the past, her fears and insecurities manifested themselves in illness and tardiness. She appeared for just one day of filming out of fifteen, resulting in a $2 million loss to the studio. Fox, stung by its financial losses due to Elizabeth Taylor's exploits during the filming of *Cleopatra*, came down hard on Marilyn. She was fired from the picture. A studio source said, "Something has to be done with these unprofessional people. We have to sit down on them or else forget about the industry. They're ruining it."

George Cukor (whom Nunnally Johnson claimed "loathed Marilyn and was given to blackguarding her in terms that would have brought a blush to Sophie Tucker's cheeks") later said of Marilyn, "There may be an exact psychiatric term for what was wrong with her, I don't know—but truth to tell, I think she was quite mad. The mother was mad, and poor Marilyn was mad...."

189

OPPOSITE A celebration of Marilyn's thirty-sixth birthday on the set, a week before her firing. The cake referred to her nude swim: "Happy Birthday (suit)."

Her last public appearance, on her birthday, June 1, 1962, at a Los Angeles Angels game. After her firing and replacement by Lee Remick, Dean Martin quit, saying he had signed to play opposite Marilyn and no one else. Fox held its ground, filing a breach of contract lawsuit against Marilyn, and a studio executive predicted it would mean the end of her career. "Marilyn claims she couldn't work because she was sick. I actually believe Marilyn thinks she's sick," he said. "It's all in her mind, of course, and maybe her mental condition makes her physically ill. I don't think she can control herself."

Marilyn spoke in her own defense during her *Life* magazine interview by Richard Meryman. She explained her fear of performing: "A struggle with shyness is in every actor more than anyone can imagine.... I'm one of the world's most self-conscious people. I really have to struggle.... An actor is not a machine, no matter how much they want to say you are."

About the Twentieth Century-Fox executive's comments, Monroe said, "The executives can get colds and stay home forever and phone it in; but how dare you, the actor, get a cold or virus.... I wish they had to act a comedy with a temperature and a virus infection. I'm not an actress who appears at the studio just for the purpose of discipline. This doesn't have anything to do with art...this is supposed to be an art form, not just a manufacturing establishment."

FOLLOWING PAGE A portrait from Marilyn's last photo session, by Allan Grant. The pictures were taken to accompany the *Life* interview, and despite claims to the contrary by some photographers, are indeed the last ever taken of Monroe.

At a party in August, Marilyn signed the guest register. Under "residence" she wrote: "Nowhere." Three days later, she was dead. The coroner's verdict was that her death was a "probable suicide" from an overdose of barbiturates.

Lee Strasberg delivered the eulogy at her funeral, from which Joe DiMaggio barred her Hollywood "friends":

"We knew her as a warm human being, impulsive and shy, sensitive and in fear of rejection, yet ever avid for life and reaching out for fulfillment....In her own lifetime she created a myth of what a poor girl from a deprived background could obtain. For the entire world she became a symbol of the eternal feminine. For us, Marilyn was a devoted and loyal friend, a colleague constantly reaching for perfection...it is difficult to accept the fact that her zest for life has been ended by this dreadful accident. I am truly sorry that the public who loved her did not have the opportunity to see her as we did, in many of the roles that foreshadowed what she would have become. Without doubt, she would have been one of the really great actresses of the stage.

"Now it is all at an end. I hope that her death will stir sympathy and understanding for a sensitive artist and woman who brought joy and pleasure to the world."

ABOUT THE AUTHORS

JAMES SPADA was ten years old when he was first enchanted by Marilyn Monroe in 1960. At thirteen he founded the Marilyn Monroe Memorial Fan Club and produced its bulletins and journals for four years. Mr. Spada is the author of the best-selling *Streisand: The Woman and the Legend; The Films of Robert Redford; The Spada Report;* and *Barbra: The First Decade* and is publisher of *Barbra,* a quarterly magazine about Streisand. His writing has appeared in numerous periodicals, including *McCall's, Us, Los Angeles,* New York *Daily News,* Philadelphia *Inquirer,* Chicago *Tribune,* Los Angeles *Times,* and London *Daily Mirror.* Born and raised in Staten Island, New York, he now lives in Los Angeles, where he is at work on his next book, a dual biography of Judy Garland and Liza Minnelli.

GEORGE ZENO's extraordinary collection of Marilyn Monroe memorabilia was recently profiled in *Life* magazine. He "discovered" Marilyn in 1953 and was vice-president of the Marilyn Monroe Memorial Fan Club for four years. Mr. Zeno is a library assistant for Time, Inc. He studied at New York's Fashion Institute of Technology and is a free-lance fashion illustrator. Born in Puerto Rico, he now lives in Manhattan, where he is at work on several media projects concerning the life of Marilyn Monroe. This is his first book.

PHOTO CREDITS